BEGOTTEN ©

A Journey of Hope

Jurlean Fowler Avery

BEGOTTEN©

A Journey of Hope

The
Fowler-Wallace & Wilson-Phillips
Family
Bienville and Winn Parish Louisiana, USA

Then - Now

The bitterest tears shed over graves are for words left unsaid and deeds left undone.
—Harriet Beecher Stowe

The Press Club Publishing Company

The
Fowler-Wallace & Wilson-Phillips
Family
Bienville and Winn Parish Louisiana, USA

Then - Now

The bitterest tears shed over graves are for words left unsaid and deeds left undone.
—Harriet Beecher Stowe

Jurlean Fowler Avery

BEGOTTEN©

A Journey of Hope

Jurlean Fowler Avery

Author

FIRST EDITION

Designed by Jurlean Fowler Avery

Library of Congress Cataloging-in-Publication Data - Applied for.

ISBN 978-1-885513-01-4

ACKNOWLEDGEMENTS

I have been greatly encouraged in this work, by the interest so many of you have shown, the information, resources, help and cooperation so many have given me. I am eternally grateful for every person I met, as well as those I became re-acquainted and reconnected with. The pleasure has been all mines.

Where names, dates, and places are noted, without any malice or intent, some people and locations may have been missed or perhaps errors in details may have been made. However, please know that every possible effort was made to capture and record as much known and accurate information and I beg forgiveness for any oversight or error, praying that you count it to my head and not my heart.

DEDICATION

For who they were to me, a Man of known, good character,
and a Woman of virtue, for all they gave to the planet,
and for the colossal love they shared,
I dedicate this work to the memory of my beloved parents.

Mamie Bessie (Wilson) Fowler
February 16, 1923 – January 28, 2007
&
Theodore Henderson Fowler
February 15, 1914 – September 12, 1997

"At the heart of every man's story.....
Is the story of his heart?"
Stephen Davey – Wisdom for the Heart

The story of my Mom & Dad's heart
Is that they loved family
And
We sincerely loved them.

PREFACE

And it shall be, when the LORD thy God shall have brought thee into the land which he sware unto thy fathers, to Abraham, to Isaac, and to Jacob, to give thee great and goodly cities, <u>which thou buildedst not</u>, And houses full of all good things, <u>which thou filledst not</u>, and wells digged, <u>which thou diggedst not</u>, vineyards and olive trees, <u>which thou plantedst not</u>; when thou shalt have eaten and be full; Then beware lest thou forget the LORD, which brought thee forth out of the land of Egypt, from the house of bondage.

Deuteronomy 6: 10-12 King James Version

I believe there is an innate need within all of us to know and understand where we came from, how we came to be, and who we are in relationship to our ancestry. Likewise, I am convinced that once we are gifted with that knowledge, we then have a responsibility to honor the lives, the sacrifices, and achievements of those who went before us; to live up to the dreams and expectations of our forefathers, and then with love and thanksgiving, pass on their experiences and lessons to future generations. The scripture's above, offers our very first and unique caution that we cannot forget who we are, we should never forget where we came from, and we must always remember that we owe all that we have, first and foremost to God, and then to those who journeyed ahead of us.

BEGOTTEN was birthed out of my own yearning to know my heritage, and far before I could complete my research, I would come to know that with this valued information, came an equivalent responsibility. I had reached a point in my life where the search to know things, learn more, understand greater, and be better had become an overwhelming quest for me. I am older, far more tolerant and yet, with regards to my genealogy, I still had so many unanswered questions. If only I could, I would run to my Mom and Dad, and read off the litany of questions that now raced through my head. Unfortunately, that is not possible; my father passed away September 12, 1997, and my mom 10 years later, on January 28, 2007. While I do credit them both for all of the history they shared with us while they were yet alive, I now realize there was still so much I wanted to know, needed to know; questions I had not before entertained, or things that previously, had not even seemed important to me. The sin of procrastination was haunting me, and the poem, "If Tomorrow Never Comes" was repeatedly playing in my head, like an old scratched record, worn and scarred by too much play, over, and over, and over again:

"If Tomorrow Never Comes"

©By Norma Cornett Marek - 1989

If I knew it would b the last time that I'd see you fall asleep,
I would tuck you in more tightly and pray the Lord, your soul to keep.
If I knew it would be the last time that I see you walk out the door, I would give you a hug and kiss and call you back for more.
If I knew it would be the last time I'd hear your voice lifted up in praise, I would video tape each action and word, so I could play them day after day.
If I knew it would be the last time, I could spare an extra minute or two, to stop and say, "I love you, "instead of assuming that you KNOW I do.
If I knew it would be the last time would be there to share your day, well I'm sure you'll have so many more, so I can let just this one slip away.
For surely there's always tomorrow, to make up for an oversight, and we always get a second chance to make everything all right.
There will always be another day, to say our "I love",
And certainly there's another chance to say our "Anything I can do's?"
But just in case I might be wrong and today is all I get,
I'd like to say how much I love you,
and hope we never forget.
Tomorrow is not promised to anyone, young or old alike,
And today may be the last chance you get,
to hold your loved one tight.
So if you're waiting for tomorrow, why not, do it today?
For if tomorrow never comes,
you'll surely regret the day,
That you didn't take that extra time for a smile,
a hug or a kiss
and you were too busy to grant someone, what turned out to be their one last wish.
So hold your loved ones close today, whisper in their ear,
Tell them how much you love them and that you'll always hold them dear.
Take time to say "I'm sorry," "please forgive me,"
"Thank you" or "its okay",
And if tomorrow never comes, you'll have no regrets about today.

છ•ఠ

And so, without further delay or hesitation, I was fixated on this path, and as much as I wanted to find names, birthdates, and lifestyles, I was so much more determined to find the story of my people, their purpose, their hopes, dreams, and what it was they would have us to know and achieve. I had to know what drove them, I believed then, as I believe now, those truths would help to lead me and others back to the path that would impel us in our purpose; A purpose that had become strangely ambiguous for some, and simply lost to others, and yet, a purpose that I somehow knew, to be real. A purpose that was calling out to us, a purpose that could not wait for an invitation, but one that we, as a people, and as a family needed to pursue right away, now, post-haste, today.

Throughout our community's, the rampant lure, use, and destruction of drugs, the apparent annihilation of individual self-esteem, spirit, and moral fiber has effectively, worked to do as much damage to us, as a people, as did the practices of slavery and Jim Crow. Mass numbers of people have succumbed to the evils and captivity of stuff, things and lifestyles that should have never even warranted our attention in the first place.

Generations worked to build ladders constructed of life, death, love, adversity, spirit and determination to help us grow, help us attain a better view of tomorrow, a clearer view of our past and a vision of where we can go. With BEGOTTEN, I sought to examine the past rungs of that ladder; the measurement of faith, the source of determination, the seed of resilience, a hope for tomorrow, hope for peace, for love one to another, and the hope of an opportunity that we might fulfill those deeds left undone.

Far more than a mere record of my ancestry, BEGOTTEN became clear and convincing evidence, that even in the midst of the most unbearable, horrific and tragic circumstances, a people entrenched with love, faith and hope can indeed abound. Whether for members of my family, your family, or complete strangers, BEGOTTEN, is far more than a journey of hope, but a prescription for vision and expectation.

If I succeed in inspiring or in any way enlightening you, I will have every reason to be satisfied with my efforts, and forever grateful for this opportunity. Further, I pray that BEGOTTEN will serve as a stimulus for both, you and I, as we journey towards the destiny that is ours.

Jurlean Fowler Avery

The Fowler-Wallace
&
Wilson-Jess/Phillips
Family
Bienville and Winn Parish Louisiana, USA

Then - Now

AND SO IT BEGAN

The bitterest tears shed over graves are for words left unsaid and deeds left undone.
—Harriet Beecher Stowe

In her poem, Harriet Beecher Stowe (1811-1896), a staunch abolitionist, and author of "Uncle Tom's Cabin" captured the very essence of what we have come to know as love and life. Love is what we feel, life is what we do, and when a life is over, the mantle of what could be, is passed to those left behind. It is when we fail to do life, when we squander away the moments of time, we then spend a considerable portion of our allotted years, grieving the undone. Like most, I too, have dismissed words left unsaid and deeds left undone, for tomorrow. Now older and wiser, I know the reality, that sometimes, "there is no tomorrow", thus I am so very grateful for this opportunity to share my story of a people, enshrined in hope.

At the first gasp of breath, a newborn baby is called to action, a call to go forth and pursue the purpose for which he/she is called into this life. While I have been able to trace the mantle of my lineage well over 100 years, it is safe to say that the journey began many, many years prior, and most likely, in a land that we know not of, and yet, it is clear that there is real purpose, and genuine destiny in the blood line I know to be family.

From the annals of history books and family narratives, the day to day life of my African American ancestors in the 1800's was harsh, to say the least. Slavery was such a horrific existence, that few of us today can even imagine, and far too dreadful for some born in that era to endure, and many did not. There is nothing that I have read, seen or heard of that period, that was good, pleasant or otherwise happy, and yet, a thread of my family line was able to capture the resilience of their spirit, and etch their way out of that horrible pit, to go forth and pursue the purpose for which they were called.

Shortly after the 1863 Emancipation Proclamation, my ancestors on both sides, pulled up roots from their slavery locations, sought and settled new homes in parts of Louisiana. According to early U.S. Census Records, Slave Schedules, and family lore, my maternal family, the Jess/Phillips line, left the shackles of slavery from a plantation in Charleston County, Charleston, South Carolina, while the Wilson line sailed from England, (*quite possibly as a result of the Trans-Atlantic slave trade*, where slaves were initially sourced in Senegambia and the Windward Coast. Around 1650 the trade moved to west-central Africa; the Kingdom of the Kongo and neighboring Angola. The transport of slaves from Africa to the Americas forms the middle passage of the triangular trade. Several distinct regions can be identified along the West African coast; these are distinguished by the particular European countries who visited the slave ports, the peoples who were enslaved, and the dominant African society(s) who provided the slaves.*) tout down roots in Atlanta, Winn Parish, Louisiana. About that same time, my paternal family (Fowler-Wallace) left their past behind at slave plantations in Stone Mountain, DeKalb County, Georgia, and Shelby County, Alabama, to make what would become their new home in Heflin, Bienville Parish, Louisiana.

The travel, the modes of travel, the hardships and hurdles of moving long distances, through strange territory's, to unfamiliar, but new land's, and where the future was unknown, had to be a massive strain, and yet, whatever the risks, regardless of the time and trouble, and no matter what the future might hold, it had to be oh, so much better than their horrific past, and so, my family, like so many others, not looking back, and without hesitation, went forth.

As one might imagine the journey from their several destinations would have taken my ancestors many days and weeks, or more to complete.

United States of America

For the benefit of our children, their children, and those of you who simply find it hard to imagine, just know that when our ancestors of the 18th and 19th century's, were making their journey from the dreads of slavery, and plantation life, the Cadillac Escalade, Toyota, Ford or Jeep that's parked in your garage did not exist; cars had not yet been invented. Since air travel had not yet surfaced either, there were no Airlines to call for reservations, no Greyhounds, Trail Ways, and not even Amtrak.

Unlike the highways and expressways we take for granted today, the travel routes and modes of the 18th and early 19th Century was extraordinarily brutal, but it was all they knew, and all they had. Horses, mules, stagecoaches, wagons, carriages, and journey by foot were "the" modes of travel.

Water travel was another important part of eighteenth-century, and ships were the only method of transportation across the Atlantic. The voyage from England to any of the major colonial American ports took an average of six to eight weeks, that is, if all went well. Ships also sailed the coastal route between American ports such as Boston, New York, Philadelphia, Norfolk, or Charleston. Of course, the least expensive and most common way to get from one place to another was by foot, so walking was the common mode of transportation for poor whites and slaves.

Please believe me when I say, the United States is not the America of television and movies. It is large, complex, and diverse, with distinct regional identities. Due to the distances involved, traveling between regions was time-consuming and expensive. Southern USA is a lush, largely subtropical region with cool, verdant mountains, agricultural plantations, and vast cypress swamps. So walking, and not always assured of their direction, through harsh and sometime deadly terrain, the pioneers of my family garnered all of the strength, determination and faith they could muster, to go forth. Without the benefit of today's GPS technology, map quest, and at times, without real directions at all, they yet, forged ahead; telling time by the location of the sun, directions by the moss on trees, being led by prayer, an unyielding faith, and sheer hope, they forged ahead.

I have tried to visualize their journey; Young, old, men, women, and children, with few provisions, some with shoes, most without, at times cold, often hot, wet, dry, hungry, anxious and yet resolute, sick in the body, and nevertheless strong in their will, often confused, but patient nevertheless. Weary but eager, unsure and yet certain, once "owned", but now alas, they were free. What could possibly compare to an existence of brutal life of servitude, to a new life of freedom, knowing that when you awake in the morning, other than God and Him alone, there was no master. Now being able to talk, discuss and share the pictured plans of your life, that heretofore could only be silent dreams and visions in your head, dare not spoken aloud. What could possibly compare to the dignity of men, and heads of families, being addressed by a proper name, rather than the slurs of former handlers. What could compare to the meager rations from man who loved you not, to the natural and wholesome provisions of God, who surely loves you. What could possibly compare to a former existence without expectation, to this, a new life of hope ever lasting? There is nothing equivalent, surely nothing that could ever measure to a horrifying past of slavery, to a future, maybe without wealth, perhaps without mansions or fine possessions, but a future of freedom. Moving from a living death to a living hope, the very realm of being free, being a free person. That alone, would be sufficient to catapult a people to a life, and a future unbound. While imagining them on the dusty roads, through swamps, hills and woods, I felt that the ever popular gospel hymn, **"His Eye Is on the Sparrow"**(reportedly written in by two white songwriters, lyricist Civilla D. Martin and composer Charles H. Gabriel), was little doubt, just one of the songs that inspired our ancestors on their journey. As they walked, and made their way under the cover of night, my very soul can hear the melody of their soft, quiet, but weary voices singing and humming......

Why should I feel discouraged; Why should the shadows come,
Why should my heart feel lonely And long for Heav'n and home,
When Jesus is my portion? A constant Friend is He: His eye is on the
sparrow, And I know He watches over me; His eye is on the sparrow,
And I know He watches me.

And they walked, and they sung

I sing because I'm happy, I sing because I'm free, His eye is on the sparrow,
And I know He watches me (He watches me) His eye is on the sparrow And
I know he watches (I know he watches) (I know he watches me)

And they walked, prayed and they sung

I sing because I'm happy, I sing because I'm free, His eye is on the sparrow,
And I know He watches me (He watches me) His eye is on the sparrow And
I know he watches me (He watches me) He watches me (I know he watches me)

And they walked, prayed, cried and they sung

"Let not your heart be troubled," His tender word I hear, And resting on His
goodness, I lose my doubts and fears; Though by the path He leadeth, But one
step I may see: His eye is on the sparrow, And I know He watches me; His eye
is on the sparrow, And I know He watches me.

And they walked further, prayed harder,
They wept, and still, they sung

Whenever I am tempted, Whenever clouds arise, When songs give place to
sighing, When hope within me dies, I draw the closer to Him, From care He sets
me free: His eye is on the sparrow, And I know He cares for me; His eye is on the
sparrow, And I know He cares for me.

And they journeyed on..........

For a people who knew little about reading, writing and formal education, it's most obvious to me that our ancestors felt, believed and somehow, just knew enough about God that, in spite of all they had endured through slavery, suffered through Jim Crow, lost, grieved and the many horrors they faced, none of their suffering was of God and in the midst of it all and beyond, they never ceased to give Him glory and exclaim God's Amazing Grace.

Satan knew that the Lord had blessed our people with enormous and magnificent gifts and resilience and for hundreds of years; he has unleashed his army of trials and tribulations in an attempt to try and destroy us. I submit to my generation, our children and their generations yet to come, _if we will just continue to praise and worship our God and give Him all the glory for His Amazing Grace, just as our ancestors endured and was brought out of the bondage of slavery, we can likewise, endure and be saved from the murderous, rampages upon our people and any other malicious crime, violence and injustice and we can for once and from here to everlasting, kill that enemy that has for so long, tried his very best to kill, steal and destroy us._

'Tis Grace that brought us safe thus far
And
Grace will lead us home.

WHY LOUISIANA?

One would presume that since our ancestors were enslaved and endured so much harshness in the South, once freed, they would move as far away from the South as possible. That's obviously easier said than done, given that for most, their sole mode of transportation was by foot, perhaps a mule and just maybe, maybe a wagon, but none of which would take them as far as I'm sure they might have truly desired to go.

Passed on July 21, 1866, the Southern Homestead Act, a United States federal law, enacted to break a cycle of debt during the Reconstruction, following the American Civil War, opened up 46 million acres of public land for sale in 160-acre plots in the Southern states of Alabama, Arkansas, Florida, Louisiana, and Mississippi. The primary beneficiaries for the first six months were freedmen who were in desperate need of land to till. Before too much land was distributed, however, the law was repealed in June 1876. I have little doubt that the Homestead Act was a major attraction for my ancestors and others.

I do recall my mother sharing a story of her family, owning land in Atlanta, Winn Parish, Louisiana, which contained minerals and timber. Likewise, I recall my father sharing a story of his family, owning land in Heflin, Webster Parish and Bienville Parish.

It is well documented, that my great-grandparents, William "Bill" and Francis Phillips became community leaders, as well as major landowners, donating approximately two acres of land in 1908, to build a school and church for the African American community in Emden/Atlanta, Winn Parish, Louisiana. "The Phillips School "constructed in 1918 and operated until 1955, was "founded on the principals that education would improve your life and your total existence". *The Phillips School; a state accredited one-room school, still stands today, is recognized and has earned its rightful place on the National Register of Historic Places.

The New Bethlehem Baptist Church (1875 – 1995) and the Phillips School, both stand on their original site of construction. The following is a history on the Phillips School.

*From: A History of the Phillips School, by Stafford Davis

In 1918, an abandoned building near the Verda area was torn down, moved, and reconstructed on the present day site to become the Phillips Schoolhouse.

The Phillips School was not your typical elementary school of today. It was founded on the principle that education would improve your life and your total existence. It was a state accredited one-room school with a wood burning heater and kerosene lamps, where the teacher was also the school's principal. It was the first and only African-American school in the Emden Community. Prior to this, school was held in the New Bethlehem Baptist Church.

The school year was from October to February, which allowed the children to beat home when needed for family farm duties. There was only one teacher at time for each school term and one grade at a time was taught while the other children studied. Even though only one teacher was available occasionally, an older student would oversee a lower grade. All grades would have class each day.

Classes consisted of the "3 R's; Reading, Riting, and Rithmetic." Spelling, geography, and arithmetic were taught daily with health class on Fridays. There was a book for each one.

Sometimes classes were alternated. To teach personal development items such as table manners, telephone use, and etiquette, although there were not telephones in the community! Mrs. Beatrice Ball would tell her students,"these are things you will need to know in the future."

The students walked to and from school, the ones from Wheeling had to cross two creeks by walking over a large tree, which were cut to serve as bridges. There were days when lunches were lost to the creek. In the late 1930s the men of the community built a small kitchen for the school. To buy the school's kitchen utensils, community mothers donated their time and food, made and sold candy and box suppers in the community. With Mrs. Ball's assistance and the older girls cooking, they were able to have ahoy meal. Meals were mostly beans and rice, commodities supplied by the State of Louisiana. However students had to purchase their milk at 6 cents per day.

This school also provided the community with entertainment. Having what was referred to at the time as "programs". But in fact, they were dramatic plays where the students were the actors. The school was blessed with well-educated teachers whose main concern was for the students to receive a well-rounded education, despite the fact of receiving only used books frequently having torn and missing pages. When pages were missing the teacher would do her own version of the story to complete it for the students.

Mrs. Dessarine Phillips-Smith recalls her first new book as being a history book, which she received after World War II, when she was a junior in high school.

The school's benefactors, William "Bill" and Francis Phillips were the parents of nine children: General Lee, Eliza, Isabella, Arlevia, Emanuel, William Jr., Napoleon Alexander, Raymond, and Lisbon. They were also very community and civic minded people. Both were born during slavery in America. In their lifetimes, in addition to being loving, caring parents, they also became community leaders as well as major landowners. She was a Deaconess and he was a Deacon, blacksmith, and dentist.

In 1908, they donated approximately two acres of land to build a school and church for the African American community. The Phillips School was constructed after the New Bethlehem Baptist Church. Today they both stand on the original site of construction. The New Bethlehem Church has been continuously active since its construction.

Mr. Morell Fobbs has profound memories of helping with the rebuilding of the Phillips Schoolhouse. Although he was a very young lad at that time he pulled nails from boards and performed other small tasks to assist in the construction. As time passed, another duty he acquired was to walk the teacher to the "doodle bug" (train) which ran from Winnfield to Aloha and back to Winnfield. It stopped at the Emden crossing approximately one mile from the Phillips School.

Among the first Phillips School board members were Jack Fobbs, Jack Sapp, and William "Bill" Phillips.

The 1954-1955 school year ended, and along with it, the operation of the Phillips School. Due to integration, school could no longer be held in the building. The school board donated the land to the Emden Community.

The Phillips School operated for 37 years in this building (1918-1955) with enrollment in 1920 of 80+ students in this one room school. Given an average enrollment of 50 students per school session it educated approximately 1,850people from the African American community.

The donation of their time, materials and the land for the Phillips School and the New Bethlehem Baptist Church, only begin to show Bill and Francis Phillips' tireless devotion. They were very concerned about the condition of their fellow man.

All former students expressed great pride in the Phillips School education they received. Many of the former students continued their education in trade schools, colleges, and became professionals in various fields.

The hard work of several former students, family members, and a former teacher, Mrs. Lula Mae Thomas was rewarded on February 10, 2000, when the Phillips School was given its correct place in American history by being placed on the National Register of Historic Places.

This building, having historic WILL, an example of what people working together can do, even if they come from very adverse conditions.

Students were from the following families:

Carter, Crawford, Crenshaw, Fobbs and sentimental value as well as great memories, also stands as a monument to FREE, Ford, Harrell, Hayes, Henry, Houston, Howard, Hunt, Johnson, London, Mathis, McCain, McMillion, McWright, Morgan, Mosley, Peats, Pennywell, Phillips, Rodgers, Sapp, Shelton, Smith, Stanley, Starks, Walker, Watkins, Willis, and Wilson.

Teacher List:

Mrs. Beatrice Ball (husband Joe Ball, Ms. Dora Robinson, Ms. Ollie L. Morgan, Ms. Maude Peats, Ms. Margaretta Harris, Rev. J. E. Hunt (did not pastor New Bethlehem Baptist Church), Rev. H. L. Thomas (did not pastor New Bethlehem Baptist Church), Professor Casey (female), Ms. Winnie Blackwood, Ms. Mary Jane Cunningham, Ms. Alberta Swafford (daughter of Ed Swafford), Ms. Mary Jane, Ms. Doris Brown, Ms. Melviney Blackwood, Mrs. Ina Mae Winslow Fobbs (husband Morell Fobbs), Mrs. Lula Mae Howard Thomas (husband Roosevelt Thomas)

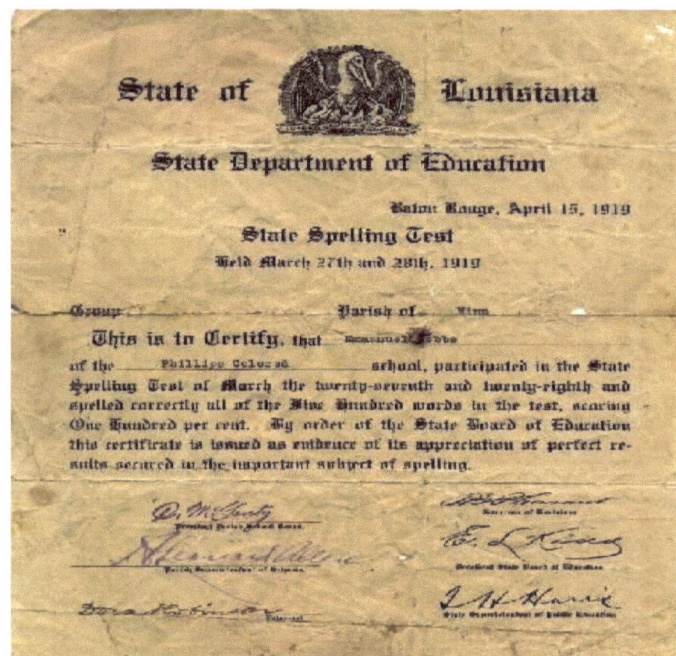

The above certificate was awarded to Emanuel Fobbs, a student at Phillips Colored School, in 1919 for correctly spelling 500 words in a two-day test. The Phillips School was located near New Bethlehem Church in the Emden Community southeast of Atlanta in southeastern Winn Parish. Morell Fobbs, Emanuel's brother, remembers Emanuel talking about the test and saying that he went blank on the last word. He said it was one of the easiest words on the test and nerves caused him to miss it. When he regained his composure, the word came to him and he found himself shouting out "S-A-U-S-A-G-E"!

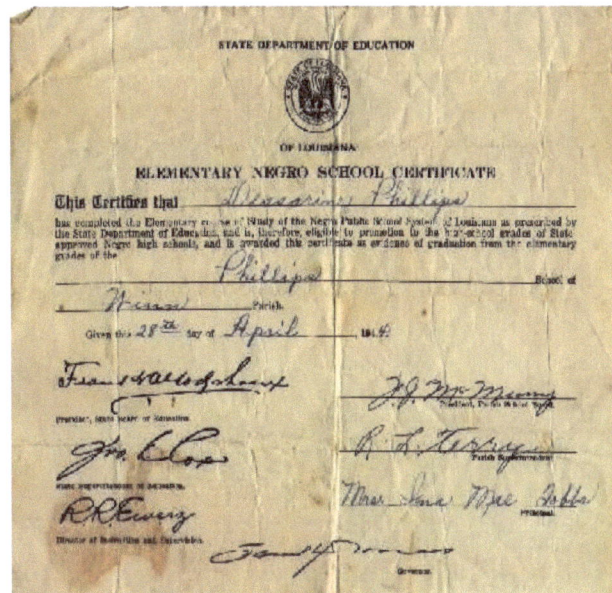

1944 Elementary School Certificate of Dessarine Phillips.
Submitted by Stafford Davis
Web page by Peggy Beaubouef, March, 2000

~Blessed~

During this time, very few Blacks could read or write, but they were convinced of the importance to learn. They had no formal religious training, but they knew if they simply talked to God, he would surely hear them. They had extremely limited financial resources, but they were diligent and responsible with what they had. So they learned, they taught, they prayed, practiced Christian values, and meditated on the Word of God. They worked, provided for their family, earned, and saved what they could.

AN ENDURING HOPE

These were a people of hope, consumed by will, inspired by the love of the one true master, the God of earth, heaven and all things known and unknown, the God who had set them free and led them out of the bonds of slavery. This was a people building a ladder of promise, for me and for you. I am overwhelmed at the very thought that over 135 years ago, my ancestors who endured so much, made enormous sacrifices, and who, so fervently valued family and life, has left us such a rich and perpetual legacy of hope, and a future where failure should never be an option.

And yet, the state and temperance that find our children and grandchildren today, while though saddening at times, leaves me nevertheless, encouraged. To see our young men and women wasting the times of their very lives to drugs, crime, and all manner of degradation is so very disheartening. To witness the very fabric of family untwine is sickening. To be in the midst of life and close our eyes to the destruction of our youth is simply shameful. To live, know, and have the comforts of some opulence and also, have a front seat to poverty is disgraceful. To pride and boast of education, degrees and achievements, and know the struggle of those who can barely read and write grants us no cause to swank. To declare that you have overcame, while knowing others have not is no victory. Just like the fervor and diligence of our ancestors, we must be convinced of the importance in knowing that the journey will never be complete until, and unless we all make it home. I cannot rest if I know that your struggle continues, and you should not be content in your success, knowing that I am yet in the midst of my voyage.

I'm hopeful, because while the experiences and trials from one generation to the next may very well be quite different, a struggle is a struggle regardless of the time or era it presents itself. I am confident in the generations of today, because they have the blood of a people of hope running warm and fresh throughout their body, because they share that same DNA riddled with promise and a strong will. Surely, after all we have been through, we cannot give up, we cannot turn our backs. Failure is not an option, and like our forefathers, we must tenaciously, go forth, putting one foot before the other, with shoes or without, under the cover of dark, and in the full light of day, when we are strong and even when we are weak, well and sick, rich and poor, hungry and full, happy and sad, rested and tired, brave and scared. No matter what the circumstances or situation, failure can never be an option. In our homes, our relationships, schools, on our jobs, and within our community's, failure simply, cannot be an option for us. Where would we be, had my people and your people, gave up on their journey out of slavery, if they refused to go on because the road was too rough and the hills were too high to climb, where would we be. Had my people and your people not persevered and gone forth when the hurdles of life reared its ugliness, I shudder to think that you and I would never have known the light of day. It is the direct result of the churches, and schools that we did not build, land that we did not toil, wells we did not dig, provisions that we did not plant or harvest, protests that we did not participate in, marches we did not walk, meetings that we did not attend, causes that we did not support, people that we did not encourage, prayers that we did not pray, tears that we did not shed, and prolific sacrifices that we did not make, that permits us to be here, to enjoy the light of this day, to have what we have, to love and be loved, to breathe, and if nothing else, to be free. So we have no right to declare defeat, failure is simply, not an option.

Most recently, I was blessed to attend a wonderful, reunion for my paternal (Fowler) side of the family, and found my way into a robust conversation concerning today's youth, school, their future, and what could possibly be the answer for some of our children who are failing to thrive in life. My nephew, Carl, a thought provoking, hardworking, dedicated man, is a master protagonist in advocating the pros and cons of such debates, and that particular day, while other participants declared and defended their opinions, Carl was very much on his mark. I was proud that these men, the heads of households of my family line, were aware, were acknowledging the existence of such problems, and investing in such a healthy debate. I was comforted just to see them together, and as I looked around the room and in the eyes of my son, my nephews, and cousins, I could feel the hope of my ancestors running through my veins, with the assurance that likewise, it was running through theirs. The whole concept of hope is a massive pipe dream, when kept to your-self and never unleashed, but when shared, intently and abundantly spread about to all in its path, hope is and can be the switch that lightens the life of a very dark existence. I am confident that a life nurtured and entrenched with hope, is a life that drugs and the pitfalls of life cannot successfully capture. I am persuaded that when we begin to make an earnest commitment and strive to live, to be, to do, to share, and totally embed our lives, with the kind of hope that it took our ancestors to endure slavery, come out of bondage, journey for days, nights and miles, travail through dirt, mud, rain, sleet, snow, heat, hunger, sickness, and fear. The kind of hope that it took our ancestors to walk unashamed, go confidently, have faith in their success, and know that their journey was not in vain. The kind of hope that they would be proud to pass on to their children, and their children's children, children, children...... The kind of hope they lived and died by, being assured that it was right and good. The kind of hope, that without it, they would surely die. The kind of hope, that would make them procreate just to pass it on. The kind of hope that make a man know what his responsibility was to God, himself, his family and life, and made him proud to assume it. The kind of hope, that made a woman understand, and treasure her virtue, and encouraged her to express it with dignity. The hope in children that nurtured the curiosity of their youth, that yearned their thirst for knowledge and made them respect the scope of their authority. The kind of hope not manufactured in 10 step programs and rehab day cares, but the kind of hope practiced, prescribed and administered in living rooms, dens, at kitchen tables, and in bedrooms of those places we call home.

Much like your ancestors of those early times, my forefathers, with a pervasive hope also had dreams and visions, and yet they knew how to be ever so grateful, and mindful to appreciate and care for all that they had at the moment. After all, they were free from the bondage of slavery, and any blessings beyond that, was simply icing on the cake. Unfortunately, that appears to be a trait quite absent from today's generation, and much of that is our own fault. While we wanted so desperately to give our children more and more of everything, all that we did not have, and everything that we missed, we failed to also share with them the gift of thanksgiving, and teach them the meaning and significance of respect. As a result, we birthed and have now raised a generation of young men and women under an elusive and pre-conceived notion of entitlement. There is a proverbial "elephant in the room", and it is little wonder that we find ourselves praying, discussing, and debating the unfortunate plight of our youth, and trying to formulate a cure for the monsters, we, ourselves, have created. I would suggest that in the course of this process, we also take a bit of time to at least, acknowledge to ourselves and to our children, that this "situation" is most partly, the result of our own making. Confession, after all, is good for the soul.

OUR PATH

African Americans have a very, unique path to follow; one that absolutely requires us to know our history, honor our ancestry, learn from all they endured, and use the lives through generations of regeneration, that is now you and I, to further, improve, and stabilize our path for generations to come. Certainly, we can and should do everything possible to improve our lot, it is very important that we broaden our perspectives, utilize every opportunity, grasp new and different concepts, learn all we can, explore new places, experience new ideas, befriend other cultures and people. And I say to you that we cannot successfully achieve any of those "new" things, until and unless we successfully understand the things and lessons of our past, otherwise, we are certain to repeat our mistakes.

Today, where freedom abounds, opportunity remains relatively, plentiful, and people across all cultures are encouraged to express themselves and reach for the stars, as a people, as African Americans, we continue to grapple with some real, but very basic problems that speak to the very root of who we are; our little Black girls still do not like themselves, how they look; their hair or skin color. Little Black boys continue the struggle to find their rightful place; lashing out, bashing, and disrespecting. Many young Black women fight with the issues of self-esteem and assimilation; spending millions of dollars each year, not simply to enhance, but to drastically change the natural beauty that is theirs. Black men have nearly lost their identity and placement in the family, while the Black family has become a mere remnant of the powerful and beautiful entity it once was, and so desperately need and deserve to be. We have effectively transferred our insecurities about ourselves to those we interact with, and as a result, people in our world think of us, and treat us, the same way we feel about ourselves. If you do not think that you are beautiful, others do not see us as beautiful. When we embrace low self-esteem, others believe that we are insecure and weak. When Black men elect to use every conceivable circumstance and excuse not to assume their place and responsibility's as men, husbands, fathers and heads of households, others see them as weak, useless, and of little value. Even in the midst of slavery, and certainly after the abolition of slavery, our forefathers wanted desperately to learn, but they could not go to school, and was forbidden an education. Today, though surely it has its flaws, Public Education is free, attaining a good education is encouraged, and yet in some major cities, nearly 50% of Black students fail to complete high school. A recent statistic reports that <u>every 26 seconds, a teen drops out of high school</u>, and that includes children in my family, and your family. At some point, we lost our way, we strayed from the path, and as a result, we have become horrendous statistics under such headings as African American children born to unmarried mothers, African American men in prison, the Unhealthiest, the Unemployed, the Uneducated, Poverty Households, etc. We have strayed far off the path. We have allowed the "stuff, things, and life-styles" of a world, so not on our path, to become so pervasive in our lives, that it has nearly glossed over the clear vision of what is real, right, moral, good and just for us. Lots of stuff, nice things, and rich life-styles, may be perfectly fine and good, in and of themselves, and for those who need and can readily afford them, but when you neither need, or can afford them, despite what the advertisers say, One Size "does not" Fit All, and "trying" to keep up with the Jones', Jacksons', Smiths', Housewives of NY, New Jersey, D.C., the rich and the famous, is simply ludicrous! Much like a cataract in an eye, the view of our real path is cloudy, so much so, that it has effectively dashed out all glimmers of hope for some, set others on a road of vice and destruction, and left still others unable to recognize their own identity. Visions of driving a Rolls Royce, when that same vision does not even include a garage and hefty bank account, is much like one of sugarplums dancing in your head and not a vision that you should entertain. Boasting about your plans to buy the latest in fashion, fine jewelry, and that $6,800.00 Vivian Alexander Bag for Christmas, as you struggle to pay the Fall/Winter utilities, is way beyond unrealistic, and "Making it rain" at the "club", when you owe child support, is so totally irresponsible.

I am convinced that if they were here today, to say from their own lips, our ancestors would tell us of the many dreams, visions and desires they continue to have for us; how they want us to have bountiful life, peace, happiness and great joy. They would confirm that on some plane, they would marvel to see us being chauffeured in that Rolls Royce, living in that estate, and enjoying all the stuff and things that would make us happy, but on another plane, far more importantly, I am absolutely convinced, that they would take more time, and great patience to stress the importance that we invest our physical and spiritual resources to assure that our men be good examples, loving husbands, great fathers, and masterful men; that our women be virtuous, decent, intelligent, decorous, genteel, polite, respectable, and seemly. They would admonish our children to enjoy their youth, and be inquisitive; learn all they can, be respectful, honor their mother and father, and they would remind them that in addition to the Ten Commandments, the old golden rule to "do unto others, as you would have them do unto you" are still "trendy" and the best guidelines for life. They would tell us that the best and only reality show that we should be watching is taking place, each and every day inside our very own homes, that the only "trends" that we need to be tracking are those we can proudly adopt or establish ourselves, and those that will not cause harm and in any way belittle, disrespect or otherwise, de-value us. The role models our children choose to admire and look to, need to emanate in their own homes, and establishing and working within realistic goals and viable priorities need to become our modes of operation. They would tell us that these are some of the landmarks on our path, these are the signs and indicators that we need to watch for to know that we are on our rightful path.

Dreams and visions are wonderful, it is admirable to have them, and we should all nurture and support them, but even dreams and visions should be maintained in their proposer perspective. Most dreams and visions depict us "getting" stuff, things, and relationships but the Reality of Life, portray our struggle to "keep" them. Just a very few years ago, when the economy "appeared" good and all "appeared well", we bought/leased fine cars, new homes, trendy fashions, and everybody had long hair, lashes, manicures, pedicures, smart phones, I-Pads, I-Pods, Notebooks and a few dollars in their pocket. Then the bottom dropped, the jig was up, and the "appearance" of what we perceived to be "well", was revealed to be the illusion it really was.

I don't have all the answers, and I admittedly, have made some of the same mistakes that many of you have, and from my own mistakes, I have learned and truly believe that if we at least begin repairing the breach within ourselves, and within the boundaries, doors, and rooms within our own families, homes and communities, separate fact from fiction, stop buying into the delusions and fantasies of this world, and re-establish the "villages" that we know it takes to raise a child, nurture our family's, sustain our relationships, live life within our means, encourage, respect, and love one another, we can then find our way back to our rightful path. A path not riddled with elusive get rich quick schemes, or pie in the sky, over the top lifestyles that have absolutely nothing to do with, or for us. As my mother, and I'm sure her mother before her use to say, "Wrong is wrong, and right don't hurt nobody". It does not take a genius for you and I to know when something is wrong or right and what just might seem right for others, is not always right for us. Discernment is the key.

The mantle was left to you and me, and there remains much work left undone and so many strive to make. The clock is ticking family. There is destiny in you and I, goals and achievements meant for us to reach, and when we stay on the path of our destiny, I assure you that all of the "stuff, things, jobs, titles, money, and life-styles", <u>purposed for us, we shall have</u>. Gospel Artist, Marvin Sapp famed a song entitled, "What God has for me, is for me", and I do believe it to be so; that the things in this life that are meant for us, can never be given or lost to anyone else, and those things destined for another, cannot be successfully, gained and held by us. The purpose for which God made us, can never be achieved by other people. It is pre-destined that you be who you are, do what you do, speak the way that you do, look the way you do, and make the marks in this life that you will. While we cannot change our ultimate destiny, some of the choices that we make, can serve to make the path that we must follow to our destiny, a bit rougher than it need be. Obviously, I am a believer in the doctrine of "Predestination <u>and</u> Free Will", of which, there is biblical support, rather than one versus the other. Quite simply, while the will of the Lord shall be done, we are given the right and encouraged to use our free will to choose good over evil, and right, over wrong. There is a path for us, and there are choices that we must make; the task before us, is to make the right choices, re-position ourselves on the path of <u>our ultimate destiny</u>, and like our ancestors, go forth. Our path may very well resemble others, but let us not mistake an illusion for reality. Let us not allow the perceptions, and dreams of others become our reality. Know what is good, right, just, and what works for you. Simply because "Economists", CNN, and your co-worker say that family's today must have two incomes to "make it". I can assure you that a very, very good percentage of what you see and hear on T.V., Radio, and even in person, <u>does not apply</u> to you or your family! Granted, there are some sacrifices that we all need to make in life, but I assure you that the welfare of our children, the stability of our relationships, the moral fiber of who we are, and the identity of the birthright, that we bring to this planet should not be up for grabs; they cannot and should never be forfeited for a chase after an illusion that someone else has superciliously convinced us that we should have, or otherwise need. Before you permit the stability of your family to be placed in jeopardy, you and your family need to define what "making it" means for you, and all of that stuff that "does not apply", needs to be dismissed, Stop trying to make it apply, when clearly, it does not, and carefully explain to your children the things that not only do not apply, but why and how they do not apply! Is leaving your minor children, unattended for prolonged hours at a time, or in the care of some stranger, or other irresponsible person really "worth", "making it"? Is reducing your marital relationship to a brief glance at your spouse, as you pass one another going to and coming from jobs, in order to buy stuff and things that do absolutely nothing to edify your relationship or your life, worth it. Can you really say that your lifestyle consists of doing the things, spending the time, going the places, investing the money, and being with the people that you do, is absolutely "the very best, right, and most just" for you and your family! When you ask yourself the following questions, and reply with genuine, honest answers:

1. Is this right or wrong?
2. Does this apply to me and my family? If so, how, and why? If not, how and why not?

If you have been honest, and can justify every sacrifice that you are making in your life, God Bless, but if you cannot, if there is even one thing that you know is not working for you and your family, or may be placing someone or something in your life in jeopardy, I encourage you to run, don't walk, back to the path of your destiny! Now, it is quite possible, that some people are unable to answer those questions for every aspect of their life by themselves, perhaps you need help, and that is what family is for. I would encourage those people to call a meeting, gather your family or trusted friend, pour out the heart of your dilemma, and ask them to help you.

**"There is a way which <u>seemeth</u> right unto a man,
but the end thereof are the ways of death."** Proverbs 14:12

LEGACY

I have no doubt that some of our forefathers made poor and at times, fatal choices, but much of what I have read, heard and learned, indicated that when important choices had to be made, the decision maker, whether man or woman, laid aside all pride, and consulted with the elders among them, family, church, or close personal relations before making a decision. The consideration was that most decisions to be made, generally presents at least, some residual effect on others; A failed marriage that ends in divorce presents consequences for people and organizations, other than the once happy couple. Irresponsible financial management will undoubtedly result in a loss to someone else. A decision of one person to indulge in the use of a habit forming drug, drop out of school, live an unedifying life, have a child as a single parent, or partake in some potentially detrimental behavior, will most likely produce lingering costs to family, friends and community, who had absolutely nothing to do with the initial choice. We are not solitary and independent in the choices we make; this is not an island, and we do not live here by ourselves; what we do or don't, evolves into a price for others, and most likely, those that we love and share a common bond with. It's a delusion to think that just because you are a grown "a__" man/woman, that you can do whatever you want – well yes, you can, but those choices you make, will affect other people, whether you intended them to do so, or not. Whether the subject of our decision is good, evil, honest or not, we owe it to ourselves, and those we love to consider the repercussions, and count up the costs of our choices. Consult with others, talk to someone you know who genuinely cares about you, get yourself a mentor, ask a caring and responsible person to be your personal life coach, but don't go it alone, don't wait to find the cat out of the bag, an elephant in the room, or no way to turn, before you realize that the end product of your choices are now the mantle you are leaving to your loved ones to carry. Let's face it; there are some legacy's that are neither, wanted or deserved. It is both, an act of love and responsibility to leave a good legacy. Because of the enormous power of our lives and the impact upon other's, it is a great responsibility to choose to leave a positive legacy. All men and women must take responsibility to create legacies that will take the next generation to a level we could only imagine. Legacies have power for good and for bad. There are people who have changed the world for good, people who have opened up new worlds for millions of others, people who have spurred others onto new heights, and then there are those who have caused massive destruction for countless millions, leaving a wake of pain and destruction behind them wherever they went. Let's be proud of the legacy that we build and leave for our children. There are parents who have blessed their children with greatness and yet others who have ruined their children's fragile minds and hearts. The legacy left to you and I, is one of powerful hope, and it is that hope that gives me the strength and confidence to know that I can face whatever comes. It empowers me, builds me up, lets me know that I am loved, that I own a right to be respected, that I can achieve, and that if, by some chance, I should fall, I can and shall get back up. Some time ago, I was asked to give a tribute during a family reunion. I prayed and diligently, sought God's leading on what, if they could, our ancestors might say, to our family at this reunion, and the following is what was birthed in my spirit to write and present:

A Love Letter to Those I Love

Written, produced and presented at the
2010 Fowler-Caldwell Family Reunion
Virginia Beach, VA.
By Jurlean Fowler Avery

I have tried to imagine in the 1800's, when my parents, grandparents, and great grandparents were but mere, starry eyed young adults, if they dreamed about the contributions they might make to the world and if they imagined the legacy they might leave. I don't know how much time they gave to such things, but somehow, some way it happened, and year-by-year, you happened, I happened, and we happened. Generation by generation we came to be, the Wallace's, Fowler's, the Caldwell's, Smith's, and so on. Family is such an awesome dynamic, and I know that it was not by sheer accident, and we did not come to be, just because. I am convinced, and I believe that our ancestors knew likewise, that we have great purpose to achieve and masterful plans to carry out. After much prayer, meditation and seeking, the words of this tribute flowed from their spirit to mine, to let you know that our ancestors yet, have great faith in us, as individuals and as a family, but more importantly to remind you just how much wearer still loved. I wanted to know what my Grandma and Grandpa, and those that preceded and have since followed them would say to us today, and I believe this is just some of what they would share.

*While there have been countless opportunities, and perhaps even many failed attempts, I may have not successfully and completely told you that I love you, just how **much** I love you, and all that you mean to me. Perhaps I tried to show you, but my actions were not sufficient, or did I say it, and my language failed short in the attempt. I love you because you deserve to be loved, I love you because you are loveable, I love you* *because you are a part of me, and it is an eternal part of my purpose to let you know not only that I love you, but just how much I do.*

I cannot imagine that you knew just how much I love you, you did not know how much I would sacrifice, that I would go to the ends of the earth for you that I cry every time you cry, or that my heart fills with joy when I know that you are happy. While I knew it would not be right, I want revenge for, and against anything, and anyone, even if it was me, whoever hurt, misused or treated you less than royalty. I ache in agony whenever you feel pain, and my spirit travail at the very notion that you face a dilemma. Each night you laid down to sleep, I want to turn your bed into a soft, heavenly, love filled cloud, to form fit your body from head to toe, and cause you to dream the dreams that dreams are made of. When you awake, I want your eyes to open up to splendors of beauty to cause you to glow, make you smile, and fill you with love. When you arise, I want you to stand with confidence, move with authority, exude grace and dignity, and spread the universe with the power of you.

I want your imprint on this life to know and remember that you were here, that you left it far better than you found it, that you made a difference, that this world will never be the same without you, and that you mattered.

*I want all of your dreams to come true, I want your touch to be gold and your gold turned to platinum. I want your jewels to be genuine, bright, rare and precious. I want all that you need and desire to be yours, **how** you want it and **when** you want it. I want your thoughts to be magical, your dreams to be real, and your opinions highly sought after. When it rains, I want the drops that touch your lips be the taste of sweet nectar; I want your hair and clothes to be water repellent, and any mud that forms around your feet to become your favorite flavor of sweet, decadent chocolate. I want your mind to travel beyond belief and straight to knowing that whatever you desire is possible. I want you to know that you are far more precious than precious, that there is no other that can, nor will ever compare to you, that you are uniquely you, you are invaluable, priceless. I want rainbows to seek you out and follow your every move, I want trees and flowers to bloom and grow simply because you are in the midst, I want babies to move in the wombs of their mothers when you are near, I want bees that fly, fish in the seas, and the fowl of* *the air to take notice of your presence and honor you with the sounds of their nature.*

*I want you to know heaven on earth **and** above. I cannot imagine that you knew just how much I love you. I want **everyone** to love you, and I want them to tell you and show you that they do. I want them to admire not only your character, but your person, your spirit, and I want you to be the ultimate role model, the standard by which virtue is measured. There is no good, and pleasurable things in this life, nor any life hereafter, that I want withheld from you. I want no fears, or trepidation to share your space in life.*

I cannot imagine that you knew just how much I love you. I want your skin to forever be smooth as butter and soft as that of a newborn baby. I want your eyes to be the jewels that let you see nothing but beauty, and all that you are to be perfectly aligned. I want your hands to mold great inventions, write great novels, and futuristic plans for the universe. I want there to be nothing about you that brings you shame, uneasiness or insecurity. I want you to be magnificently and wonderfully you. I cannot imagine that you knew just how much I love you.

I pray, meditate and I worry about you daily. You are always on my mind, forever in my thoughts, and permanently etched in my heart. What brings me great joy is knowing that you are joyful, what makes me feel love is knowing, that you are loved, and what makes me fulfilled is knowing that you are complete. I sleep less and less each night, anxious about the opportunity to await and witness the joy that you are sure to bring to the planet each day. I cannot imagine that you knew just how much I love you, but love you this much, I do.

*I want the best day of your life to be **every** day of your life. I want your greatest pleasures to be **all of your pleasures**, and your most memorable achievements to be your **entire life.** I want all that you hear to be a symphony to your very soul. I want the lyrics of songs and tones of music to flow with magic and stream with beauty in the very event that you might hear. I want you to invent, create, design, and discover. I want creation to marvel at the unbelievable prominence that is you. Every time a new team is formed, beyond the teammates, the captains, and coaches, **you** own the team. Whenever a new business or organization is birthed,* *without question the Chief Executive Officer shall be **you**, the head, the boss, the lead, the authority, **you are it**. Before the beginning of alphabets, **you** are listed; ahead of all numbers, **you** are noted; and at the top of everything with a heading, **you** are the header. You are all that you are and can ever imagine yourself to be, you are all that I want you to be and can ever envision you to become. I believe in you, I have faith in you, and I cannot imagine that you knew just how much I love you. My love for you is deep, it is wide, and indeed my love for you is immeasurable.*

I pray, profound blessings with abundant joy for you, I want for you peace, love, opportunity, and all that you can ever ask and hope for, and if you can permit your mind to just imagine it, if you will simply allow your heart to open and receive it, I want our Lord and Savior, who loves you even more than I, to pour you out a blessing that will simply consume you.
~ 2010 ~

I don't know of a greater legacy, I can't quite imagine a more wonderful gift that my ancestors could have possibly left our family that would surpass the love and hope I know they had for, and gave to us. Our lives have the power to create good or supply evil, and it is imperative that we choose the very best, the most powerful, enduring, and positive good that's possible. In spite of their many claims of endurance, that expensive bag, game toy, shiny new car, and trendy clothes will only serve our children but an elusive moment, the next season, or until the newest trend come along. Mothers and Fathers, let us journey into our history with confidence that the path we laid for our progeny is built on the surest foundation, with strong, durable tools and materials. Let's assure them that the path laid for them will serve the generations of our family to the coming of Christ Jesus, let's comfort them with the knowledge that our life was lived with a perspective of the "big picture" that included them, their children, and their children's children.

Purposefully leaving a legacy for others breaks the downward pull of selfishness that can be inherent in us. When we strive to leave a legacy for ourselves, we are acting with a selflessness that can only be good for us. Working to earn and donate money to assure your moniker on some plaque or building, while perhaps commendable, is not the kind of legacy I speak of. Legacies that make life better for those who come after us, not about our own celebrity, but about helping others far beyond the span of our lifetime. To build that which will last beyond us is selfless, and living with that in mind breaks the power of selfishness that works so desperately to employ itself in our lives. I refuse to believe that your ancestors and mine endured the institutions of slavery, servitude, and Jim Crow, out of their own selfishness, but rather, with a sight of the "big picture", a canvass of love, and a masterpiece of hope, that included you and me. There was an easier way out; they could have quite simply, chose to die. Rather than endure the beatings, savage treatment, witness the rape and torture of sisters, wives, and daughters, live and sleep in huts and hovels not befitting human life, being bought, sold, and bred like animals, surely death would have been preferable, easier, and of course, patently justifiable, but there is no glory in giving your life to one who neither, deserves or loves it. Life is to be fought for, protected, and shielded. Our ancestors preserved their life, in order that they might give life to you and I. Robert South, an English Churchman said, *"If there be any truer measure of a man than by what he does, it must be by what he gives."* The legacy we leave is part of our ongoing foundations of life. Those who came before left us the world we know and live in. Those who follow us will have only what we leave them. We are responsible to leave our future generations a world, better than we found it. When mold our children understand, cherish, and pursue a good life, built on righteousness, service, honor, faith in God, humility, sound knowledge, love, far beyond looks and popularity, now that's a legacy to be proud of. When we help our girls to know, without a shadow of a doubt that they are beautiful, valuable, precious, and honored, simply because "they are", and not in comparison to someone else, or as a result of long hair, make-up, fashion, or trends, that's a legacy of immeasurable value. When we aide our boys in learning the worth that is within them, and cease the struggle and search of an identity that is not theirs, the foundation of our path will surely strengthen. When our Black Men, determine that absolutely, no matter what, they are going to stand, and be Men, be the sons, brothers, husbands, fathers, and the heads of households that we so desperately need them to be, that's a legacy assured to last an eternity.

When we make up our minds to come together, as a family and as a people, to honor our ancestry, remember and learn from our past, take pride in ourselves, diligently live each moment, invest in sacrifices, show respect, give respect, have respect, appreciate every blessing, "Do what we can, with what we have, where we are", harm no one, help one another, be kind, and with love, do unto others, as you would have them do unto you. When we help build <u>that</u> kind of life, the one that gives the gift that keeps on giving, generation after generation, now that's a LEGACY.

RELATIONS & RELATIONSHIPS

Just as important as it is to know our relatives, both immediate and distant, it is just as vital to have and maintain relationships with them. All families have a "family tree". a tree comprised of individuals who were/are, I believe, divinely placed there, either by birth, adoption or marriage, to live out their predestinated purpose and it becomes the responsibility and function of the other members (leaves) in that tree to help nurture and support one another towards the achievement of their purpose. If, as most families have now become, we allow ourselves to become ignorant, distant and/or simply uncaring of those in our family tree, the tree itself, lacks its required nutrition and eventually die. Years ago, living far distances from our relatives represented an unfortunate hurdle to establishing and maintaining contact with our relatives, but with the invention and availability of current technological resources and alternate means of transportation, it has never been easier to locate, reach out, establish and maintain relationships, leaving very few excuses. It should not matter, no, it <u>cannot</u> matter whether 1 mile or 1000 miles separate us from our relatives, we still have a responsibility to nurture and support one another towards our God given purpose. When we look at the state of our families today, they are dying: failing to thrive as a result, of a lack of nutrition. The kind of nutrition derived from love, encouragement, support, education, enlightenment and communication. Granted, family reunions are wonderful opportunities to <u>help</u> address that responsibility, but annual or bi-annual reunions are simply not sufficient to adequately, address the nutritional needs and requirements of most families today. Just as the popular online site, "LinkedIn" permit us to build and engage professional networks with business professionals and associates, our very own "Family Tree" should be and is a gateway for us to communicate and support one another. As our children, grandchildren, and their children grow, enter this world and its varied environments of schools, universities and work places, they should and need to know that they have their very own personal "network", made up of aunts, uncles, nieces, nephews and cousins all over this country and abroad that they can count on and call upon for that nutrition ("love, encouragement, support, education, enlightenment and communication"), they so desperately require. We should never need to, nor have the desire to look <u>outside</u> of our tree for role models, heroes, and mentors. To know our loved ones are looking to sports, music, entertainers, actors, fashion and other celebratory types as their role models, heroes and leaders, is quite simply a slap in our faces and should alert us that something is drastically wrong. I submit to you that all of the role models, idols, leaders, mentors and advisors we will ever need can be sufficiently located right in our own "Family Tree". I challenge each reader to reach out, research, locate, make contact, build and maintain close and meaningful relationships with those in your tree. It's important, it's absolutely vital.

Over the years, I have noted that there are <u>numerous</u> talented "Writers" in my family and I am convinced that writing is just one of many God given gifts bequeathed to us and yet, as a "Family", there has been very little effort to nurture those gifts. I'm not referring to the occasional compliment we give one another but rather an organized and comprehensive resource within the family, designed to foster, encourage and support those gifts. I implore every member of my maternal and paternal family to become more diligent towards 1. Building and maintaining relationships with those in our tree, whether near or far, and 2. Nurturing the gifts that live, and breathe in, and among our tree. Let's not allow the books, stories, plays, screenplays and other gifted masterpieces die and be buried, without ever having the opportunity of fulfillment.

When we truly nurture our relations and relationships, we also nurture those gifts within. The hyphen, which is so aptly, found between the date of birth and date of death for each individual should represent the "purpose" of that life. It is not just a line spaced between those dates, without reason or cause, but a defining measurement that points to the fulfillment of the purpose for which he/she, was placed on this earth. Why should we allow our tree to die, when we can so easily give it life, in our relationships, one relative, one to another?

Date of Birth – Date of Death

REUNIONS

Unlike many families, I am quite proud that over a period of 36 years, since 1978, my paternal family (Fowler-Caldwell), has consistently hosted biennial family reunions, all across the USA.

1. 1978 Toledo, OH
2. 1980 Dallas, TX
3. 1982 Detroit, MI
4. 1984 Las Vegas, NV
5. 1986 Las Vegas, NV
6. 1988 Chicago, IL
7. 1990 Shreveport, LA
8. 1992 Los Angeles, CA
9. 1994 Houston, TX
10. 1996 New Orleans, LA
11. 1998 Chicago, IL
12. 2000 Detroit, MI
13. 2002 Shreveport, LA
14. 2004 Crystal City, VA
15. 2006 San Diego, CA
16. 2008 Toledo, OH
17. 2010 Virginia, Beach, VA
18. 2012 Biloxi, MS
19. 2014 Austin, TX
20. 2016 Scheduled for Atlanta, GA

Initiated by my beloved, late uncle Johnny Fowler, our family reunions have grown and progressed throughout the years. Now that our patriarchs and matriarchs have fulfilled their earthly purpose and passed the mantle to us and the generations that follows, the responsibility to strengthen and sustain the bonds of family, while trying at times, is nevertheless ours and not to be taken lightly. I am proud that the younger generations have been remarkable in stepping up to this challenge.

For many African Americans, the union of faith and family have historically, been tightly bound together. Unfortunately, the 21st century has revealed an unraveling of not only the bonds of faith and family, but many other strong ties that once kept our families together. Other than the funeral of beloved matriarchs or patriarchs and maybe family reunions, few people make it a priority to host or participate in activities that help maintain and support family ties. This neglect has been a contributing factor to the resulting pervasive weakening of our family units. Obviously, economics, employment obligations and other structured lifestyle responsibilities play significant roles in the barriers that divide and hinder us. Most family reunions are hosted annually or biennially and with multiple choices of transportation resources currently available, our resolve to support and participate in family reunions, in particular, need to be far greater. We are resourceful and creative people who can transform reunions into events that are affordable, inviting, fun, entertaining, educating, inspiring, wholesome, valuable and memorable moments. Family reunions can and should be far more than food, games and fellowship but can and should be a significant opportunity and resource for health, education and economic empowerment for the family. Sure, I know what you are thinking, "that sounds like a lot of work". Yes, you are absolutely correct, but then, anything that is worth doing is worth doing right, and that generally entails a lot of work. The end result however, is that the benefits can be amazingly wonderful.

In researching my ancestors, various documents gave me solid proof of certain historical health conditions that seem to be prevalent, even now, throughout both sides of my family. Diabetes, Heart Disease, Hypertension and Anemia are some of the chief causes of death that were noted on many of the documents I located on relatives. Knowledge of the commonness of such medical maladies throughout our family is so important in educating and helping current and future generations towards proactive lifestyle changes to eliminate those illnesses in our gene pool and it issues such as this that should have a platform at our family reunions. The saying that, "When we know better, we should/can do better", is a perfect fit here. When we are educated concerning issues that can help, improve and in some instances, save our very lives, we should use that information to do better. Granted, lifestyle changes are seldom easy, but they can be done and with the support and inspiration of "family", who love, care and want only the best for us, we can do it.

Throughout our family, we have educators, attorneys, financial experts, counselors, medical professionals, writers, business owners and many other professional experts with skills, knowledge and the ability to help other family members achieve their dreams and goals. Networking, supporting and mentoring within our own family tree can only result in much stronger and dynamic roots for generations to come. In their own unique ways, it is what our ancestors did and I am quite certain, that it too, is what we must do. Given that even in our modern day and times, unfortunately, there are still very, very limited resources for African Americans to turn to for genuine help in certain areas, so I find it simply outlandish, to have such a bounty of viable resources on our "own family tree" and allow the fruit to spoil. And so, in this effort to encourage families, in general and my family, in particular, I pray that you forgive me for repeating those infamous words of the late and beloved Maya Angelou, *"I did then what I knew how to do. Now that I know better, I do better."* **Family, let us do better.** Let us not just have Family Reunions, make certain that we show up and let's have **"FAMILY REUNIONS".**

BEGOTTEN

I am so very proud to present the
Generations of
A People of Hope

The Fowler-Wallace & Wilson-Jess/Phillips Family

Bienville and Winn Parish Louisiana, USA
Then - Now

PATERNAL FATHER	PATERNAL MOTHER	MATERNAL FATHER	MATERNAL MOTHER
FOWLER	**WALLACE**	**WILSON**	**JESS/PHILLIPS**

JURLEAN FOWLER

Our Names

*"The name we give to something shapes
our attitude toward it."- Katherine Paterson*

There are several biblical cases where a person's name was changed by God. In those instances, it seemed that it was usually to establish a new identity and to represent the plans that he had for their lives. The new name meant something important. Examples of this is when God changed Abrams name, which meant "high father", to Abraham, meaning "father of a multitude" and his wife Sari, which means "my princess" to Sarah, "mother of nations". He changed Simon's name, which meant, "God has heard" to Peter, meaning "Rock"

Years ago, when babies were born, considerable prayer, time and attention was expended to naming the new child. A surname is usually inherited, while given or first names are more important in a way because they not only represent a voluntary choice, but a reflection of the thought, feelings and hope of God and the parents. From his/her inception, the given name becomes a defining trait for the child, a testament to God and the parents or person that named him/her.

In today's culture, more often than not, we do not see the same names used over and over again in families. While certain names are popular in different areas in different times in history, the repetition generally represents a pattern. Many cultures believe in honoring their elders and do so by naming children after them. The new baby might be named after a parent, grandparent, other member of the family, or cherished friend.

While it does not appear to be as important today to some, there was a time when it was very important that the given name "meant" something; it needed to have some relevance, it had to be suitable, and worthy. Giving a baby a name, with a befitting meaning would be one of the primary seeds placed in his/her life. Thus, a baby named Mary, which means *"my beloved*" or *"my love"*, represents a lifetime of affection each time Mary hear or states her name. A seed of love was planted in her at birth, and should she retain her given name until the end of her life, a lifetime of love will grow and nurture within her. It was not only important that the newborn be given a relevant and befitting name, but it was equally important that as the child grow, and mature, the meaning of the name should be continuously taught and reinforced.

Unfortunately, the celebratory practice of naming a child is not given the scope and attention it once was. Many people today, have a vague, or no idea of what their name means, and very few young parents, unfortunately give them little thought. When people refer to the "meaning of a name", they are most likely referring to the etymology, which is the original literal meaning. Given names used by Blacks are often invented or creatively spelled variants of more traditional names. Some names are created using fashionable syllables, for example the prefixes *La-* or *De-* and suffixes like, *isha,* and *p*unctuation marks like apostrophes and dashes. While I don't see this practice as particularly wrong, though some do argue that having a "Black-sounding" name could hurt a child in the long run. Using data covering every child born in California over a four-decade period, Roland Fryer, Jr., assistant professor of economics at Harvard University and assistant director of Harvard's W.E.B. DuBois Institute for African and African American Research, and who co-authored the study, "The Causes and Consequences of Distinctly Black Names", says no negative causal impact on life outcomes, were found from having a distinctly Black name.

I simply pray that whether we elect to create, invent, or use a traditional family name, know that if there is even the most, minor chance that it may negatively define and impact your child for the rest of his/her life, please re-think it. Is it sufficient for your child to grow up <u>only</u> knowing what they are called, without any knowledge or explanation behind it and do keep in mind;

<u>"The name we give to something shapes</u>
<u>our attitude toward it."</u>
Katherine Paterson

"A good name is more desirable than great riches; to be esteemed is better than silver or gold." Proverbs 22:1 NIV

While researching my ancestry, their names, and meanings of names, this journey took on a whole new level of excitement. In preparing the following record of my lineage, you will note that following each name, the meaning of each name, if it is known, is recorded in parenthesis. As to our surnames;

My PATERNAL FATHER: **FOWLER**
Fowler meaning bird-catcher, ultimately derived from Old English *fugol* meaning "bird".

My PATERNAL MOTHER: **WALLACE**
WALLACE, meaning "Welsh" or "foreigner"

MY MATERNAL FATHER: **WILSON**
WILSON, meaning "The son of", "will", "desire", "helmet", and "protection"

MY MATERNAL MOTHER: **JESS/PHILLIPS**
JESS, meaning "gift" or "to behold"
PHILLIPS, meaning "friend"

I worked with great anticipation in search of the meaning of each name, and with great pride, I was considerably honored to learn that, judging by the meaning of their names, I descended from a line of some abundantly loving, strong, and considerate human beings.

Let us remember that Names are important.
They have significance – they define us.

My Maternal Line
The Wilson's

WILSON, meaning "The son of", "will", "desire", "helmet", and "protection"

Of My Mother's Father

My eldest documented ancestor, my great-great grand-mother, **Dilsy Powell,** (Meaning "sweet")was born 192 years ago, in 1818 in Virginia. The only two records of her existence, was found in the 1). 1870 U.S. Census, as a widow, living in Atlanta, Winn Parish, Louisiana, Ward 6, with her five children; her daughter, Sallie, 18 years old, her eldest son, Plenty, 20 years old, son, Jim, 16 years old, son, General, 14 years old, and son, Scott, 6 years old. She was then recorded ten years later, in the 2). 1880 U.S. Census, as a 62 year old widow, still residing in living in Atlanta, Winn Parish, Louisiana, but now living with her now, 28 year old daughter, my great grandmother, **Sallie (Powell) Wilson**, (Means "lady" or "princess"),born 1852 in Atlanta, Winn Parish, Louisiana, and her 30 year old, son-in-law, my great grandfather, **Henry Wilson** (Meaning "home ruler"),reportedly, born in England*, and died October 22, 1922, Atlanta, Winn Parish, Louisiana. Since no additional records were located of her after the 1880 U.S. Census, I have to assume that she died between 1880 and 1890.

Obviously, I never actually, met my great-great grandmother, Dilsy Powell, never even seen a picture of her or the name of her late husband, I could not locate a record of her death, and while there is 133 years between our births, I yet believe, that I know her, nevertheless. I believe that she was a strong, but unassuming soul; wise far beyond her years, meticulously observant, greatly discerning, kind, soft spoken, and true to the meaning of her name, "sweet". I think she shared a strong love and commitment to her family, cherished her days of freedom with them, and when content that her loved ones would be just fine, my great-great grand-mother, Dilsy Powell went on to be with her Lord.

　　Bethlehem Cemetery was earmarked as our family resting place, and I have little doubt that this is where she was laid.

Dilsy Powell
"Sweet"
1818 – God's Time
~Resting In Certain Peace~

Although the gate sign reads "Bethlehem 1950", there are many graves here before 1900. The old stones are mixed with the new in this large cemetery. Some graves never before marked now have new stones.

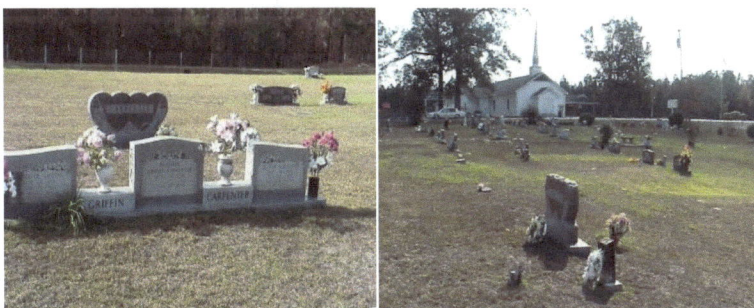

Bethlehem Cemetery Located in Ward 8 of Hwy. 1232, Winn Parish, Louisiana

The Progeny of Dilsy Powell

Sallie Powell (Meaning "lady" or princess) born in 1852 in Atlanta, Winn Parish, Louisiana, to Dilsy Powell. In 1874, Sallie married Henry Wilson (Which means "home ruler") was born about 1847, reportedly from England, and died October 22, 1922, in Winn Parish, Louisiana. They beget eight children: Kate, Lydia, Lizzie, Ida, Mary, Tom/Thomas, Gus, and Robert.

   Note: (The progeny of Sallie and Henry will follow
        under the heading of the Wilson's)

Plenty Powell ("More than adequate") born in 1850, in Atlanta, Winn Parish, Louisiana, married Elizabeth Perry ("my God is an oath"), born March, 1856. True to his name, Plenty and Elizabeth beget 12 children; Virginia, Owen, Addie, Jane, Charley, John, Fred, Oliver B., Bloomer, Lola, Bobby, and Octavia.

> Virginia ("maid", "virgin"), born in 1874, in Atlanta, Winn Parish, LA. On December 31, 1890, she married Van Shelton ("marsh", "fen").

> Owen ("youth"), born in 1876, in Atlanta, Winn Parish, LA., On September 11, 1897, he married Emma Walker ("whole", "universal"), born about 1877, and they beget 5 sons, Henry, Owen, Jr., Lawrence, Alvin and Randall; 3 daughters; Lucy, Ollie and Jesse Bell.
>> Henry ("home ruler") was born 1896, in Winn Parish, Louisiana
>> Owen, Jr. ("youth") was born 1900, in Winn Parish, Louisiana
>> Lawrence (From the Roman cognomen *Laurentius*, which meant "from Laurentum". Laurentum was a city in ancient Italy), was born 1908, in Winn Parish, Louisiana
>> Alvin ("friend") was born 1909, in Winn Parish, Louisiana

Randall ("rim of a shield") was born 1911, in Winn Parish, Louisiana

Lucy ("light") was born 1899, in Winn Parish, Louisiana

Ollie ("olive tree") was born 1904, in Winn Parish, Louisiana. She married Henry Dixon ("home ruler"), born about 1901, in Louisiana. They beget one son. James ("will, desire", "helmet, "protection"), born in 1918.

Jessie Bell (gift), was born1914, in Winn Parish, Louisiana, and died at the tender age of 6 years old, on September 27, 1920 in Natchitoches, LA.

Addie ("noble"), born in 1878, in Atlanta, Winn Parish, LA., married 1). Sam Henry Tyson ("name of God", "God has heard"), on December 25, 1895. They beget 4 daughters, Rozelia ("rose"), Luginia ("famous warrior"), Orelia ("light of God"), Lula ("famous warrior"), and raised Addie's sisters (Bloomer) infant son, Edgar Tyson ("rich", "blessed"), when her sister died in childbirth. Addie then beget three daughters; Eula L. Powell ("to talk well", "good"), Lula Tyson ("famous warrior") and Leona Tyson ("lion"). Addie then married 2). Payton Jones ("an English surname, a place name, meaning "Paega's town"), born in 1882, and they beget three daughters; Rebbie ("springtime"), Eunice ("good victory"), and Edna ("pleasure").

Rozelia was born in 1896 in Winn Parish, LA.

Luginia was born in 1898, in Winn Parish, LA.

Orelia was born January 20, 1903 and died July 29, 1953. She married Wiley Jackson and they beget one son, Morrell.

Morrel was born September 30, 1926 and died January , 1966

Lula Tyson was born in 1906

Leona Tyson was born in 1910

Edgar Tyson was born in 1909, in Winn Parish, LA. and died Feb, 5, 1987 in TX. He married Hattie Mae Pickens, born Oct. 9, 1919, in Jefferson, TX and died December 31, 2008. Hattie is survived by one daughter, Peggy Pickens of Houston; one sister, Esther Hawking of Jefferson; and two grandchildren.

Eula L. Powell was born in 1913

Rebbie was born in 1917

Eunice was born in 1921

Edna was born in 1923

Jane ("Yahweh is gracious"), born in 1880, in Atlanta, Winn Parish, LA.

Charley ("Man") bore in 1882, in Atlanta, Winn Parish, LA. On April 13, 1902, in Winn Parish, he married Emma Jackson ("whole", "universal"), and they beget 9 children; Ina ("chaste"), Charlie ("man"), Amie ("beloved"), John ("Yahweh is gracious"), Sam IV ("name of God", God has heard"), and four currently living (though unknown to this writer) children.

     Ina, born in 1904
     Charlie, born in 1905
     Amie, born in 1906
     John, born in 1908
     Mary, born 1911
     Joe L., born 1914
     Sam IV, born in 1920 and died 1987

John ("Yahweh is gracious"), born in 1884, in Atlanta, Winn Parish, LA.

Fred ("peaceful ruler"), born in 1886, in Atlanta, Winn Parish, LA.

Oliver B. ("olive tree"), born August 6, 1888, in Atlanta, Winn Parish, LA. and died 7 Jun 1955, *in* Louisiana. He married Eliza Brown ("my God is an oath", "my God is abundance"), born 1899, and they beget 7 children; Roberta ("bright Kisier ("hair"), R.D. ("thunder"), Edward ("rich", "blessed", "guard"), and Gertrude ("spear of strength").
Roberta was born Sep 2, 1912 in Trichell, Natchitoches, Louisiana, United States and died 2 Nov 2002 in Waskom, Harrison, Texas, United States
Annie was born in 1919
Emily was born in 1922
Kisier was born in 1924
R.D. was born in 1925
Edward was born in 1927
Gertrude was born in 1929/1930

Bloomer ("flower"), born in 1890, in Atlanta, Winn Parish, LA., and died in 1909. In 1906, she married Walter Tyson ("ruler of the army"), born March 5, 1883 in Winnfield, LA and died February 28, 1972 in Monroe, Ouachita Parish, LA. Bloomer died in childbirth, with her 1 son, Edgar Tyson ("rich", "blessed", "spear"), born in 1909 in Winn Parish, LA., and died February 5, 1987, in Houston, Texas.

Lola ("sorrows"), born April, 1893, in Atlanta, Winn Parish, LA.

Bobby ("bright fame"), born in 1895, in Atlanta, Winn Parish, LA.

Octavia ("eighth"), born August, 1897, in Atlanta, Winn Parish, LA., died Jun 1980, in Pineville, Rapides, Louisiana

James (Jim) Powell ("will, desire", "helmet, and protection"), born in 1854, in Atlanta, Winn Parish, LA. married Emma ("whole". "universal"), born in 1856 in Louisiana, and they beget 13 children; Henry("home ruler"), Anna ("favour", "grace"), Elizabeth ("my God is an oath"), William("will, desire", "helmet, and

protection").
    Emma ("whole", "universal"), Edward ("rich", blessed", "guard"), Preston ("Priest town"), Alick ("defending men"), Manuel ("God is with us"), Coleman ("dove"), Earl ("nobleman", "warrior"), Nellie M. ("torch", "moon") and Lucy E. ("light")

Henry, born November, 1876, in Atlanta, Winn Parish, LA.

Anna, born November, 1879, in Atlanta, Winn Parish, LA.

Elizabeth, born September, 1882, in Atlanta, Winn Parish, LA.

William, born March, 1884, in Atlanta, Winn Parish, LA.

Emma, born May, 1885, in Atlanta, Winn Parish, LA.

Edward, born September, 1887, in Atlanta, Winn Parish, LA.

Preston, born August 20, 1888, in Atlanta, Winn Parish, LA., married Carol/Edie and they beget Preston, Jr. and Ina.
    Preston, Jr. was born 1917
    Ina was born 1919

Alick, born February, 1890, in Atlanta, Winn Parish, LA.

Manuel, born November, 1891, in Atlanta, Winn Parish, LA.

Coleman, born October 20, 1892, in Atlanta, Winn Parish, LA., died Jul 1977 - Winnfield, Winn, Louisiana He married Bethel Odessa aka (Bettie O)., born in 1899, and they beget 8 sons; CHARLES, OSCAR COLEMAN AKA O.C., VAL PAL, NARVIN, HASTING, PRESTON, DONALD RAY, and BOBBY.

On May, 21, 1975, the following article was written by Vernon Ray Davenport, Sr. and published in the Winn Parish Enterprise News-American about Coleman Powell's success in raising 8 boys.

Success: Raising Eight Boys Into Talented Young Men

"It is a blessing to raise one boy to manhood, but it is an extraordinary blessing to raise eight boys into strong, healthy, talented men. That is exactly what one man who lives at the intersection of South Jones and South Pineville Streets in South Winnfield has done.

Coleman Powell, an 82 year old retired millworker, raised eight boys while earning only 9 to 15 dollars per week during the depression and afterward. He also had a truck patch, whenever he could convince someone to let him use their land.

He is the father of a former National Football League player, a nationally known soul recording artist, a manufacturer, a church deacon, two former deputy sheriffs, a city patrolman and land developer. One son is a successful businessman, owning a store and a Laundromat.

The Powell name was synonymous with great football players for three generation with seven of the boys excelling in the sport.

Preston, the sixth son, made All-State in both football and baseball while in high school. He went on to make All-American at Grambling State University before playing in the National Football League with the Cleveland Browns. Preston now makes his home in Cleveland, Ohio, where he is a deputy sheriff.

Charles, now deceased, was a deputy sheriff in Dallas, Texas, for several years after he starred in football at fullback at what was the Winn Parish Training School.

Hasting, the fifth son, was one of the greatest running backs in the history of Winn Parish. Called "Hurricane" Hasting because of his speed, he was also a great punter. He is a deacon in church now.

Val Pal, the third son and Oscar Coleman aka O. C., the second son, were also good football players. Although they did not finish high school, they showed potential of becoming great. Van Pal is now deceased and O. C. is living in Chicago.

Donald Ray, the seventh son, owns and operates a successful shop, which manufactures burglar alarm equipment in Los Angeles.

Narvin, the fourth son, was one of the first of his race to become a city patrolman in Winnfield. He also is the first of his race to own a Laundromat. Additionally, Narvin
owns a store, which his wife and children operate. The former football standout is also a land developer.

Bobby, the eighth son, is a nationally known soul-recording artist. Although blind since early childhood, he writes most of his songs. Bobby, who now lives in Baton Rouge where he finished high school, is responsible for such recordings as "Do Something For Yourself", "Red Sails In the Sunset", "The Bells", part 1 and 2, "Nothing Takes the Place of You", "Our Love", "C. C. Rider", "Question", "Peace Begins Within, Wake Up People", and his current smash hit, "I Want To Thank You".

Asked why his sons have been so successful, Mr. Powell said, "I always taught my boys to strive to be the best in whatever they do. I told them never do anything to make me ashamed of them. Anybody could whip my children when they saw them doing wrong. If they would act like they didn't like it, I would give them another whipping when they arrived home.."

Narvin added "My father always had control of his home. He didn't raise us on rules that he got from a book; he made his own rules and stuck to them. I try to use the same principles in my home," the police added. Mr. Powell said that he would rather raise boys than girls because boys are handy. "They could help me on my farm."

Asked what advice he gave his boys to make them the outstanding men they are, Mr. Powell said, "I raised them up in the church and taught them to lead a Christian life."

He said that only Bobby and Preston showed signs of outstanding talents when they were growing up.

"I could tell that Bobby was going to be a musician because he always was playing around with the piano and singing. Preston always had a ball, which he would play with every day. The other boys didn't show any special interest while they were growing up."

CHARLES, Deceased
OSCAR/OSKER COLEMAN AKA O.C., (Chicago, IL), born 24 Aug 1928, *in* Winnfield, died 11 Jun 1993 *in* Winnfield. He married Miss. Latchie and they had 2 children.
VAL PAL, Deceased
NARVIN ALEX., SR., Patrolman with the Winnfield Police Dept., born July 23, 1932, died September 26, 1992 in the line of duty at 61 years old, in Winnfield, LA., shot and killed while arresting a burglary suspect.
> Family members listed at his residence are Jean C Powell and Louretta C Powell
> Narvin A. Powell, Jr. is listed as a resident of Hodge, LA., with Winnie Powell
HASTON, Deacon in church
PRESTON Jr., Cleveland, OH, Deputy Sherriff; Born September/October 23, 1936 in Winnfield, LA.
DONALD RAY, (Burglar Alarm Equipment Co, DLA., CA.)
BOBBY (Musician, Winnfield, LA)
> Minnie L Powell ("will", "desire")
> Timothy Anthon Powell ("honoring God")

Lucy E., born in 1898, in Atlanta, Winn Parish, LA.
Earl, born January, 1899, in Atlanta, Winn Parish, LA.
Nellie M., born May, 1901, in Atlanta, Winn Parish, LA.
General, born December, 1856, in Atlanta, Winn Parish, LA., On February 1, 1888, he married Rebecca Bazadier, born in 1870, in S. Carolina, and they beget 7 children;
> Oscar, born July 1883, in Atlanta, Winn Parish, LA.
> Sarah, born July, 1886, in Atlanta, Winn Parish, LA.
> James, born September 1889 in Atlanta, Winn Parish, LA.
> Arthur, born January, 1895, in Atlanta, Winn Parish, LA.
> General, Jr., born February, 1896, in Atlanta, Winn Parish, LA.
> Juda, born May, 1898, in Atlanta, Winn Parish, LA.
> Hager, born January, 1900, in Atlanta, Winn Parish, LA.

Scott Powell, born in 1869, in Atlanta, Winn Parish, LA.

Henry Wilson (Meaning "home ruler") was born about 1847. It is reported that he migrated from England, settled in Winn Parish, Louisiana, and died October 22, 1922, in Winn Parish, Louisiana. In 1874 Henry married **Sallie Powell (**Meaning "lady" or "princess"), born 1852 in Atlanta, Winn Parish, Louisiana. They beget eight children: Kate, Lydia, Lizzie, Ida, Mary, Tom/Thomas, Gus, and Robert.

> **Kate Wilson** ("each of the two") born January, 1878. On December 22, 1898, she married Holcomb Ford ("kingfisher"), born in 1865. They beget 4 children;
>
>> Beatrice ("voyager", "traveler"), born 1904
>> Mack ("son"), born 1906
>> Leon ("lion"), born 1908
>> Mary ("wished for child"), born 1910
>
> **Lydia Wilson** (Means "from Lydia" in Greek was a region on the west coast of Asia Minor. In the New Testament this was the name of a woman converted to Christianity by Saint Paul.)**,** born in 1880. She beget
> 2 sons, Emanuel Sapp, (meaning "God is with us") born in1893 and Albert Wilson (meaning "noble", "bright") born in 1898. On June 19, 1902, Lydia married Reuben Howell ("behold, a son") and together they beget 7 children, Emanuel Howell born1899, Virda Howell born in1900, Edger Howell ("rich", "blessed") born in 1902, Henry Howell ("home ruler") born in 1904, Lee Howell ("clearing") born in1908 and died in 1970 in Midland, TX, Luella Howell ("famous warrior") born in 1910 and Mary Ella Howell ("beloved").
> **Lizzie Wilson** (A diminutive of ELIZABETH, meaning "my God is abundance") born in 1881
> **Mary Wilson** (*my* "beloved" or *my* "love") born November, 1887 in Atlanta, Winn Parish, Louisiana. She married (1) unknown; (2) Joseph Foster; Mary and Joseph beget 4 daughters; Maggie ("pearl"), Mattie ("gift of Yahweh"), Flara (Flower") and Jacks ("YAHWEH is gracious"). Mary married (3) Shedrick aka "Shed" Mathis; they beget 9 children;
> Susie M. ("Lily, Rose") born 1903, Katherine P. ("Pure") born 1914, Florsie ("Prosperous") born 1914, Josephine ("He will add") born 1917, Edward ("Guard") born 1918, Thomas ("Twin") born 1921, Roy ("Red") born 1927, Mayell ("Great") born 1934 and Mandy

("Loveable or Worthy of love") born 1928. Mary then married (4) James McCain, born in Winn Parish, Atlanta, Louisiana, son of James McCain and Laura Goff (Feminine form of the Late Latin name *Laurus*, which meant "laurel". This meaning was favorable, since in ancient Rome the leaves of laurel trees are used to create victors' garlands).

Tom/Thomas Wilson (Means "twin"), and ironically, he married a twin, and he and his wife became grandparents and great-grandparents of twins. He was born about 1889, in Atlanta, Winn Parish, Louisiana; died June 17, 1953, in Cullen, Webster Parish, Louisiana; buried in Bethlehem Cemetery, Winn Parish, Louisiana. On February 6,1903, in Winn Parish, Tom married Eliza "Liza"(Jess) Phillips (Twin) (Is a short form of Elizabeth, and means "my God is abundance"), born 4 Jan 1875 in Atlanta, Winn Parish, Louisiana; died in Atlanta, Winn Parish, Louisiana, September 6, 1930, buried in Bethlehem Cemetery, Winn Parish, Louisiana. She was the daughter of William (Jess) "Bill" Phillips Senior and Francis Peats. Eliza and Steve Jackson beget a daughter, Ernest Jackson. After Eliza's death, Tom later married Nettie (Hebrew diminutive of Hannah, meaning "favour" or "grace") in Cullen, Webster Parish, Louisiana. Tom and Eliza beget 9 children: Dock, Clarence, Ira, Gradie, Andrew David (AD), Naversha, Ida/Ila, Bessie Lee, and Mamie Bessie

Ernestine Jackson aka Ernest J. married Elijah Crenshaw and they beget Virgie Lee, born June 8, 1931 and a son, Henry born in 1936.

Virgie Lee married Jacob Mills. They beget several children, including; Jacob, Jr. Reginald R. and Shone M. Henry beget a daughter, Eddie Ruth, who married her brother-in-laws brother, Morris Mills.

Dock (Means "optimistic"), was born April 20, 1902, and died April, 1958 in Pontiac, MI. He married Ruby Alexander (Simply means "ruby" from the name of the precious stone), and they beget 2 children: Garlene J., and Alton R.

Garlene J. (From a surname meaning "triangle land") born 1939. Garlene beget Eric Glenn Wilson (means "ever", "always" and "ruler").

She married Kenneth W. Johnson (Meaning "handsome").

Alton R.(From an Old English surname, which Was derived from a place name meaning "town at the source of the river"), born March 19, 1949 and died Easter Sunday, April 16, 2006.

Clarence (From the Latin title *Clarensis* that belonged to members of the British royal family. The title ultimately derives from the name of the Clare River in Ireland),was born May 24, 1900 in Atlanta, Winn Parish, Louisiana, and died November 21, 1978 in Highland Park, MI. Clarence married Mabel Morgan (A form of AMABILIS, a late Latin name meaning "lovable"), born November 16, 1902 in Atlanta, Winn Parish, LA., and died January 21, 1986. They beget 8 children: James (Derived from the name JACOB, meaning "holder of the heel" or "supplanter", and "may God protect".), Margaret (Meaning "pearl"), Ruth (Meaning "friend"), Jessie Maude (A derivative, meaning "YAHWEH is gracious"), Clyde (From the name of the River Clyde in Scotland, which is of unknown origin. It became a common given name in America in the middle of the 19th century, perhaps in honor of Sir Colin Campbell (1792-1863) who was given the title Baron Clyde in 1858), J.C. (A derivative of Augustus or Gus, and means "great"), Lucille (Means "light"), and Annette (Meaning "favor" or "grace"). Prior to his marriage to Mabel Morgan, Clarence beget a son, Odell, born April 9, 1924 in Louisiana and died July 9, 1976 in Clarence, Natchitoches, Louisiana .

James Wilson (Derived from the name JACOB, meaning "holder of the heel" or "supplanter", and "may God protect"), born September 17, 1927 in Atlanta, Winn Parish, LA., and died April 3, 1999 in Highland Park, MI. James married 1. Velma Nash ("will", "desire") of Pineville, LA., they beget 1 daughter, Addie Mae Wilson Vercher (Meaning "noble" and "kind"), he then married 2. Millie (Means "strength") James and Millie had no children together.

Addie Mae Vercher (A diminutive of Adelaide and meaning "noble", born August 27, 1947 and died

February 2, 2001 in Pineville, Louisiana. She beget one son Carlos Latrell Vercher ("man") born 1970, in Pineville, Louisiana. He married Naomi (meaning "pleasantness") and they begot two daughters; Ashley and Yazmine.

Margaret (A derivative, and means "pearl"), born August 1, 1930, in LA. and died July 29, 2003, in Shreveport, LA. She married Joe Nash (Means "he will add"), and they beget James Earl (Derived from the name JACOB, meaning "holder of the heel" or "supplanter", and "may God protect".), Mary Ann (*my* "beloved" or *my* "love), Linda (Means "soft" or tender"), and JoAnn (A variant and means "to be" or "to become").

James Earl married Norma (Means "northman"), and they beget 2 daughters, Chaunda Means "fierce, hot, passionate"), and Shameka (Short form of Michal, and means "brook").

Chaunda married/divorced Smith (Smitty) and they beget one daughter, Taylor ("To cut").

Shameka (aka Mica) married Aaron Davenport and they beget one daughter, Paige ("servant").

Mary Ann ("beloved", "love") married Robert Valentine, II. ("bright fame") and they beget Djuana, Robert, III ("bright fame"), and raised JoAnn's son, Darcy Lydell Nash (" From an English surname, which was derived from Norman French *d'Arcy*, originally denoting one who came from Arcy in France.") following her death.

Djuana born August 12, 1969, married/divorced 1. David English ("Beloved") and they beget 1 daughter, Celeste Margaret English ("Heavenly"), born March 14, 1995 and 1 son, Victor Alexander English ("Conqueror"), born February 24, 1997. Djuana married 2. Vertis Hawkins ("Brave") and

they beget twins, Ethan ("Solid", "Enduring") and Eliece Hawkins ("My God is abundance"), born August 1, 2000.
Robert III was born September 14, 1974
Darcy born June 14, 1975 and Raffell Meeks ("God has healed") beget son, Kameron Lydell Nash ("Crooked nose") born October 23, 1995. Darcy married Frances Jeanette Green Maywether ("French man")

Linda married/divorced John Sullivan, Sr. ("YAHWEH is gracious") and they beget John, Jr. ("YAHWEH is gracious").

JoAnn beget Darcy L. Nash. She married Mr. Rayford and they had no children. JoAnn passed away on September 11, 1981 at 4:40 p.m., in Shreveport, Louisiana. Following JoAnn's death, her son, Darcy was raised by JoAnn's eldest sister, Mary Ann and Uncle Robert Valentine, Sr.

Ruth ("friend") married Robert Williams ("bright fame"), and they beget via adoption, Jeffrey L. ("peace").

Jeffrey married Juanita C. and they beget a son and a daughter

Jessie Maude Wilson ("gift") married Norman Bell and they had no children

Clyde (previously mentioned) married Vernell and they beget Lesia

Lucille ("light") married Clyde Webb and they beget Carol Lee ("song" or "hymn")

Carol Lee beget Nathaniel

J.C. married Vera

Annette Marie beget Marsha Renay Little (Meaning "male") and Terrance Wilson

Ira (Meaning "watchful") born February 16, 1909, and died April, 1975. He married Clara Wise ("clear, bright, famous"), and they had no children. It was reported that Ira did have a son, Ira, Jr., by an unknown female.

Gradie (Means "noble") married Lucy Snow ("light") of Hayneville, Alabama, and they blended a family of 4 children; one son, Alvin Wilson ("friend"),prior to his marriage to Lucy, and her daughters, prior to her marriage to Gradie, Jessie (gift), Velma ("will, desire", "helmet, and "protection"), and Anna Marie ("favor" or "grace").

Andrew David (AD aka Son) (Meaning "man"), was born July 15, 1926 in Atlanta, Winn Parish, LA. He was born with Cerebral Palsy. In the mid-1950's, he was brought to Pontiac, MI to live with his sister

Mamie B. Andrew D. never married or had children. He died in a nursing facility in Coldwater, MI, he died January 20, 1965, though the place he is buried is still unknown.

Naversha ("A Native American name, meaning "girl") born 1916 and died in 1964. She married Mr. Capers and they had no children.

Ernest J. ("serious") born 1896 and died in 1964

Ida (Means "earth") born 1895, married Elbert Bowie, Sr. (Meaning "noble" and "bright"), and they beget 12 children; It is reported that 2 children died in infancy and 1 daughter, Elijah, born in 1931died as a result of an accidental drowning around the age of 9 years old. The remaining 9 children are ("hale", "healthy"), Henry Hall ("home ruler"), Annie Mae ("favour", "grace"), Mary Lee ("beloved"), OC ("wealthy", "fortune"), Elbert, Jr. ("noble", "bright"), Evernell ("ever in life"), Lanell ("clearing") and James aka Jessie ("holder of the heel").

OC/Otis ("wealth, fortune") born 1929 in Atlanta, Winn Parish, LA. and died March 30,1984, in Detroit, MI. He married Jeanette ("YAHWEH is gracious") and they beget 2 children; Nycole Lyon ("victory of the people") and Kyer Dion ("narrows, channel, straits") born in 1966.

Nycole Lyon

Kyer Dion was born May 26, 1966 in Detroit, MI.

Elbert, Jr., ("noble" and "bright") married Lucille, and they beget 2 daughters, Evelyn ("desired") and Suizetta A. ("lily").

Suizetta beget 1 daughter, Tangina Bowie ("Dancer", "The Angel")

Evelyn married Michael Cross, Sr., ("who is like God") and they beget Michael Cross, Jr.

Michael Dewayne Cross, Jr. ("who is like God") was born August 8, 1981 in Detroit, MI and died September 11, 2013 in Detroit, MI of a heart attack

Lanell ("belonging to God"), beget Darrell Bowie ("fruitful, fertile"). Lanell 1. married Benjamin Wilson, Sr. ("Son of my right hand") and they beget Benjamin Jr. ("Son of my right hand"), 2. Married John McCurdy ("YAHWEH is gracious") and they beget 2 sons, Johnell Benjamin ("YAHWEH is gracious") and 1 daughter, Jennifer ("Fair, white, smooth")

Darrell ("Clearing") beget 2 son's, Darrell Jr. ("Clearing"), Desmond ("South munster") and 1 daughter, Danielle ("God is my judge")

Darrell, Jr. ("Clearing") beget 1 daughter, Imani ("Faith")

Benjamin, Jr. ("son of my right hand") beget Jeanean ("YAHWEH is gracious")

Jeanean beget Jeremiah McGhee ("YAHWEH has uplifted") and Morgan McGhee ("Sea, circle")

Johnell beget Shei'nell Latrice ("Pipe"), Johnell Benjamin ("YAHWEH is gracious"), Terrell ("To pull, stubborn"), Marcell ("God of war") and Amarell ("To sparkle")

Shei'nell beget 1 son, Draden McCurdy ("Noble, strength")

Jennifer beget Jasmine McCurdy ("Fragrant flower") and Richie McCurdy ("Power, rule" and *hard* "brave, hardy")

James (aka Jessie) Sr., born in 1953 (meaning "holder of the heel" or "supplanter", and "may God protect"), married Cassie Diane Chesney ("To shine"), born in 1953 and they beget one son, James, Jr. (meaning "holder of the heel" or "supplanter", and "may God protect"), born June 26, 1974 and one daughter, Brandee ("Burnt wine"), born July 12, 1980.

Brandee beget 3 daughters; Jazmine ("Fragrant flower"), born July 26, 2001, Alexys ("Helper or Defender"), born August 13, 2009 and Ayriel ("Lion of God"), born November 13, 2011

Henry H. Hall ("home", "power", and ruler"), was born January 16, 1922, in Atlanta, Winn Parish, LA. He died April 19, 1974 in a car accident and is buried in Bethlehem Cemetery, Atlanta, Winn Parish, LA. It is reported that Henry beget 2 children, though their names are not known.

Annie Mae ("favor" or "grace") born in 1926 married Sid Rison ("Wide island") and they beget 4 children, Sid, Jr. ("Wide island") Leroy ("The king"), Ida Mae ("Work, labour") and Barbara ("Foreign").

Mary Lee (A derivative, and means "pearl") born June 18, 1928 and died August 18, 2004. She married John Austin ("YAWEH is gracious") and they beget 3 children; Johnnie

Mae ("YAWEH is gracious"), John Austin, Jr. ("YAWEH is gracious") and another son, who is now deceased.

Johnnie Mae, born in Winnfield, Winn, Louisiana, married 1. John Austin and they beget 2 children, Gwen ("White, fair, blessed") and Consuelo aka (Connie) ("Constant, steadfast")
2. Kenneth Morissette ("Handsome") and they beget Kenneth Morissette, Jr. ("Handsome"). She married 3. Phillip Ocon ("Friend, lover") on June 20, 2012.

Gwen born May 9, 1964 in Natchitoches, Louisiana married Mr. Ratliff and beget 4 children, including Andrea Nelson and 6 grandchildren

Consuelo born November 9, 1972 in Natchitoches, LA., married Mr. Reed and they beget 2 children; 1 son, Raelon ("Advice") and 1 daughter, Caelon ("Slender")

Evernell ("Boar, battle") born abt 1928 in Atlanta, Winn, Louisiana married/divorced Lloyd Shaw, Sr. ("grey") and they beget daughter, Lynn ("Soft", "tender") and son, Lloyd, Jr. ("grey")

Elois ("Hale, healthy") married 1) Thomas John Pikes (Twin), 2) Mr. Payton. She and Thomas John Pikes, Sr. beget 8 children;

Jessie Mae Lewis (Gift)

Jessie Mae beget 1 daughter, Patreka Lewis (Noble)

Jessie Lee (Noble)

Jessie Lee married Dennis Jones (Shine or sky) and they beget 2
daughters; Devalorie (To be strong) and Malika (Queen)

Willie Mae (Win, desire, protection)

Willie Mae beget 1 son, Fredrick Pikes (Peaceful ruler)

Thomas J. II, (Twin)

Thomas married Carylon J. Young (Song or hymn) on August 17, 1977 in Harris County, Texas and they beget Thomas J. Pikes, III (Twin), Candace Nicole (Queen mother), April Monique (To open) and Tangie (Dancer, The angel)

Candace married/divorced Bobby McCray, Jr. on March 14, 2000, divorced Oct 16, 2007 in Houston,

Harris County, TX

Roger (Fame and spear)

    Roger married Cherie H. Dempsey (Darling, beloved) and they beget Rodrick (Famous, power)

Ronald (Advice, counsel, power, ruler)

    Ronald married Sheila R. Williams (Blind) and they beget Jaiden (Victory)

Sandra (To defend or help)

    Sandra married 1. Mr. Short, 2. Riley Batiste (Rye clearing). Sandra beget Shakera (Handsome, pretty) Marilyn (Wished for child)

        Marilyn beget 2 sons; Robin Taylor (Bright fame) and Merrick Pikes (Leader)

Bessie Lee ("my God is abundance") born April 5, 1905 in Atlanta, Winn Parish, LA. and died January 13, 1991 in Houston, Harris County, TX. She married Willie (Bud) Garfield Hayes ("will, "desire", "helmet, and "protection"), born October 10, 1880 and died July 15, 1973. They beget 2 daughters, Clara ("clear, bright, famous"), and Betty ("my God is abundance").

    Clara (previously mentioned) born 1926

    Betty (previously mentioned) married Corrie Lee Lyons (Roman family name which possibly derives from the Latin element *cornu* "horn". In Acts in the New Testament Cornelius was a centurion who was directed by an angel to seek Peter. After speaking with Peter he converted to Christianity, and he is traditionally deemed the first gentile convert), and they beget

        Von Decarol ("shield"), born August 31, 1957 in Harris County, TX.

        Corrie Lee, Jr. (Twin) ("horn"), born August 5, 1958

        Corlis Ann (Twin) ("army", "warrior"), Born August 5, 1958

        Corlis beget Jonae Corlis, ("dove") born January 21, 1987

        Christopher Sidney Booker, ("bearing Christ") born October 27, 1993

        Victor Real ("victor"), born May 2, 1965

Craig Vincent ("rocks"), born December 2, 1972
Mamie Bessie ("wished for child")born February 16, 1922, in Atlanta,
Louisiana, she died January 28, 2007, in Pontiac, Michigan. Mamie
married Theodore Henderson Fowler ("gift of god") born February 15,
1914 in Bienville Parish, Louisiana, he died September 12, 1997, in
Pontiac, Michigan. Mamie and Theodore beget 4 children; Twins,
Charles James (Twin) ("man", /"army", warrior"), Churley Gene (Twin)
(meaning "bright clearing"), Betty Gene ("my God is abundance"), and
Jurlean ("rule of the spear", "soft", and "tender").

Charles (Twin) ("man"), born February 16, 1948, in
Pontiac, Michigan, died October 11, 1990, in Pontiac,
Michigan, he never married. He beget 3 children;
Antonio Lamar Ashford, Sr. (Italian form of the Roman
name *Antoninus*, which was derived from *Antonius*.
There were several early saints named Antoninus,
including the patron saint of Sorrento. This was also
the name of a 2nd-century Roman emperor), born
Chicago, IL., Carlos Eugene Fowler*, (Spanish form of
Charles, meaning "man", "army", "warrior") and
Tameeka Bates ("beautiful" and "child").

Antonio beget 3 children; Late Antonio L. Jr.,
who died in infancy. Antonio and Charity Lemke
beget one daughter, Lexus Zariah Ashford
("helper" or "defender"), born March 7, 1995 in
Chicago, IL. In May, 2012, Antonio married Tina
Chatman and they beget 1 daughter, Abregail
Antensia Lameria Ashford.

Lexus and Nicholas Adamski beget Liam
Nicholas Adamski born, November 26,
2014 in Chicago, Cook County, Illinois

Carlos married Timica Miller ("beautiful" and "child"), and they blended a family of 6 children; Marquise Fowler (From a noble title which was derived from the Old French word *marchis, meaning* "march", "borderland", which originally referred to someone who ruled on the borderlands of a realm), Mya Fowler (A derivative of Mary, meaning "my beloved" or *"my* love"),"Ja'Nya Monay Miller" ("noble, generous"), Malik Miller (Means "king"), Naseer Fowler (Meaning "helper") and Christopher Fowler (Meaning "bearing Christ", derived from *(Christos)* combined with *(phero)* "to bear, or to carry". It was used by early Christians as a metaphorical name, expressing that they carried Christ in their hearts).

*Carlos Eugene Fowler later changed his surname to Muhammad

Tameeka ("beautiful" and "child"), beget 1 son, Tristan (Old French form of the Pictish name *Drustan*, a diminutive of DRUST. The spelling was altered by association with Latin *tristis* "sad". In Celtic legend Tristan was sent to Ireland in order to fetch Isolde, who was to be the bride of King Mark of Cornwall. Instead, Tristan and Isolde end up falling in love), and raised her 2 cousins; Joy Bates (Simply from the English word *joy*) and JaNyce Dunbar (Meaning "YAHWEH is gracious").
Churley (Twin) ("bright clearing") and Willie D. Hawkins ("will, desire" and "helmet, protection"), begot 1 daughter, Michelle Marie Hawkins (From the Hebrew name *(Mikha'el)* meaning "who is like God?". This is a rhetorical question, implying no person is like God. Saint Michael was one of the seven archangels in Hebrew tradition and the only one identified as an archangel in the Bible) born "May 2. 1968. Churley married/divorced 1. Robert Lee Brown ("bright fame"),

they had no children together; 2. John W. Moore (A derivative and meaning "YAHWEH is gracious"),and they had no children together.

Michelle (previously mentioned) married/divorced Michael Jackson (From the Hebrew name *(Mikha'el)* meaning "who is like God?") and they beget Brittany (A derivative and means "gracious, dear") born in Tallahassee, Florida and Brandon (A derivative, meaning "prince") born in 1996, in Tallahassee, Florida.

Brittany and Larry Brown (From the Roman cognomen *Laurentius*, which meant "from Laurentum". Laurentum was a city in ancient Italy), begot 1 daughter, Lauren Marie Brown (From the Roman cognomen *Laurentius*, which meant "from Laurentum". Laurentum was a city in ancient Italy), born March 29, 2014, in Tallahassee, Florida.

Betty (previously mentioned) married/divorced 1. Edwin Dwayne Byrd ("descendent of DUBHÁN", which means "dark" or "black"), and they beget 7 children; Mark Alan (Meaning "male"), Janice (A derivative, meaning "YAHWEH is gracious"), Lisa (A short form of ELIZABETH, meaning "my God is abundance"), Marshalynn (Meaning "male"), Karmen ("song"), Charles James ("Man") and Eric Keith ("Ever", "Always", "Ruler"). Betty married 2. Frank Brown ("Frenchman"), they beget no children together.

Charles born April 18, 1967 and died April 18, 1967 and Eric born August 22, 1971 and died August 24, 1971 both, died in infancy.

Mark (previously mentioned) married Tova Daniel (Means "good"), and they beget Mark Jr. (Meaning "male"), Quamaine (A derivative of the ancient Hebrew name KENAN, meaning "possession". He was a son of Enosh and a great-grandson of Adam in the Old Testament). Quaniqua (A Hebrew derivative mean "dedicated").

Mark Jr. (previously mentioned) born January 8, 1984 in Pontiac, Michigan, 1. married/divorced Mariesha (A derivative, and meaning "my beloved" or "my love), they had no children. Mark and Lataya Herrod beget a son, Maverick Alan Byrd ("independent"), born Saturday, March 28, 2015 at 6:12 AM (6 lbs 12oz), in California.

Janice (previously mentioned) married Carl Rice, Sr. (Meaning "man"), and they beget one son, Carl Jr. ("man"), born October 24, 1987 in Ft. Leonardwood, Missouri and one daughter, Jasmine Renae (From the English word for the climbing plant with fragrant flowers, which is used for making perfumes. It is derived from Persian *yasmin),* born February 21, 1993 in El Paso, Texas

Marshalynn (previously mentioned), married/divorced Dion Johnson *(From Greek (Dios)* meaning "of ZEUS", or "of the sky"), and they beget Whitney Nicole (Derived from a place name meaning "white island"), and Myles Allen (Meaning "gracious").

Lisa (previously mentioned) and Eli Pittman beget DAndre Pittman ("man").

DAndre married Kesha Paul and they beget Austin Carter Pittman, (Means "great" or "venerable", derived from Latin augere "to increase".), born March 9, 2013;

Lisa and Tony Daniel beget DaVonte Daniel (Means "fawn" "stag", or "ox"). Lisa and Anthony Watkins ("English form of the Roman family name *Antonius,* which is of unknown Etruscan origin. The most notable member of the Roman family was the general Marcus Antonius (called Mark Antony in English), who for a period in the 1st century BC ruled the Roman Empire jointly with Augustus. When their relationship turned sour, he and his mistress Cleopatra were attacked and forced to commit suicide, as related in Shakespeare's tragedy 'Antony and Cleopatra' (1606)) beget Deja Watkins (Means "already" from the French phrase *déjà vu* meaning "already seen"). Lisa married Tony Minus (Italian form of the Roman name *Antoninus*, which was derived from *Antonius*. There were several early saints named Antoninus, including the patron saint of Sorrento. This was also the name of a 2nd-century Roman emperor) and they beget no children together.

Karmen (previously mentioned) and Harold Peterson beget one son, Jayden ("thankful" or "he will judge")

> Charles James was born April 18, 1967 and died in infancy on the same day, April 18, 1967.

Jurlean (previously mentioned) and Larry Pilgrim (From the Roman cognomen *Laurentius*, which meant "from Laurentum". Laurentum was a city in ancient Italy), beget 1 son, Andre' LaVelle Fowler (Meaning "man). Jurlean married/divorced 1. William Robert Fuqua ("will, desire", "helmet, and protection"), and they had no children together. On September 3, 2011 in Virginia Beach, VA. She married 2. Charles Curtis Avery, born May 29, 1945 in Waynesboro, Mississippi.

> Andre' (previously mentioned) married/divorced Lisa Black (A short form of ELIZABETH, meaning "my God is abundance"), and they beget Mia Kennedi Black-Fowler, September 26, 2007 in Detroit, MI (A derivative of Mary, meaning "my beloved" or "*my* love").

Robert Wilson ("bright fame") born April, 1890, in Atlanta, Winn Parish, Louisiana, married Fannie, born about 1888. Robert and Fannie ("French man") beget 6 children;

 Guss ("constant, steadfast", "great", "venerable", and "to increase") born 1911

 Arthur ("man") born 1912

Earl ("nobleman", "warrior") born 1914

Gladys ("country") born 1916

Ruth ("friend") born 1917

Hellen ("torch") born 1919

Ida Wilson ("work" or "labor") born January, 1891, in Atlanta, Winn Parish, Louisiana. Ida married Mr. Teal, and they beget a son, Merity/Marty ("pearl"), born in 1907, and a daughter, Willie ("will", "desire", "protector"), born in 1909.

Gus Wilson (Meaning "constant, steadfast", "great", "venerable", and "to increase"), born in Feb., 1892, in Atlanta, Louisianan and died October, 1962. Gus married (1) Mary Tamp ("my beloved", or "My love"), born Christmas day, Dec 25, 1891 in St. Maurice, Winn Parish, Louisiana; died 30 Oct 1982 in Winnfield Hosp., Winnfield, Louisiana; buried 6 Nov 1982 in Bethlehem Cem., Atlanta, Louisiana; Gus and Mary beget eight children; Sallie Mae ("lady" or "princess"), Revirchy ("flowing body"), Jewell ("precious"), Newt ("new town"), Dutch("saint"), Tom ("twin"), Lillie M. (" symbol of purity"), Robert Lee ("bright fame"), Perry ("son of Henry"), and Kelly ("bright headed"). Gus then married (2) Kittie Sapp ("pure") in Winn Parish, Atlanta, Louisiana, born 1 Sep 1890 in Atlanta, Winn Parish, Louisiana; Kitty died 19 Mar 1981 in Atlanta, Winn Parish, Louisiana; She was buried 22 Mar 1981 in Bethlehem Cem., Atlanta, Louisiana. Kitty was the daughter of Louis Sapp ("famous warrior") and Mandy Harris ("lovable, worthy of love").

Sallie Mae (previously mentioned) married Jay Davenport ("victory") on March 1, 1931, and they beget six children, 18 grandchildren, 19 great-grand children, and five great-great-grandchildren: Jimmy Davenport("may God protect") preceded her in death; Versie ("true"), Vera("true"), Lonnie Davenport("noble" and "ready"), Dorothy Long("gift of God"), and Lillie Mae ("symbol of purity").

Jimmy (previously mentioned) married Donzell ("fertile upland")

Versie (previously mentioned) married Willie Huffman ("will", "desire", "helmet" "protect").

Vera (previously mentioned) married John Luckey ("may God protect').

Dorothy (previously mentioned) married Kary

Long, Jr. ("descendant of Ciardha" or "black").
Lillie (previously mentioned) married Dewayne
Holmes, Sr. ("dark" "Black")

Revirchy ("flowing body"), born July 3, 1915, in Winn Parish, LA.,
died September 15, 1993, in Winnfield, LA. She married Mr. Knox

Jewell ("precious") married Joycie
Newt ("new town"),
Dutch ("saint"),
Lillie Mae ("symbol of purity") married Mr. Walker
Robert Lee ("bright fame") married Willie
Perry ("son of Henry")
Kelly ("bright headed"), married Dorothy
Tom ("twin")

My Maternal Line
The Jess/Phillips Line
JESS, meaning "gift" or "to behold"
PHILLIPS, meaning "friend"
Of My Mother's Mother

Eliza (Jess) Phillips (Short form of ELIZABETH, and meaning "my God is abundance"),born in slavery, in 1835 in Charleston County, Charleston, South Carolina; She died Dec 4,1928, in Winn Parish, Atlanta, Louisiana. She married (1) unknown, and beget 3 children prior to her 2nd marriage, and they were, William (Bill) Phillips, Sr. ("will, desire", "helmet, and protection"), Laura Phillips (Feminine form of the Late Latin name *Laurus*, which meant "laurel". This meaning was favorable, since in ancient Rome the leaves of laurel trees were used to create victors' garlands), and Edith Phillips ("rich, blessed"). Eliza then married (2) Jack Sapp ("YAHWEH is gracious") in Winn Parish, Atlanta, Louisiana. Jack was born in 1825 in Georgia, and died in Louisiana. Eliza and Jack Sapp beget 6 children: Louis (meaning "famous warrior"), born 1864, Kitty ("each of the two"), born 1867, Ben (Which means "son of the south" or "son of the right hand"), born 1870 and died in 1940, Gerry ("rule of the spear" and "rule") born 1871, Eli ("ascension", "my God"), born 1873, Rosana (meant "bright" or "dawn") born 1875 and Elvira aka Elvy ("all" and "true") born 1877.

William (Jess) "Bill" Phillips Senior, (previously mentioned) born March 1857 in Charleston, Charleston Count, South Carolina; died 1920 in Atlanta, Winn Parish, Louisiana; buried 1920 in Bethlehem Church, Winn Parish, Louisiana.

Bill recalled their last name being "Jess" ("gift" or "to behold"), during slavery. Family history has it that shortly after the abolishment of slavery, Bill his mother and two sisters joined a group of people named Phillips ("friend"), that were moving from South Carolina to Louisiana. During this period, they changed their names from Jess to Phillips. It is believed, that "Jess" may have been the surname of their former slave owner.

In 1874, Bill married Francis Peats ("Of French", or "Frenchman"). She was born Mar 1858 in Louisiana, died 22 Jun 1910 in Atlanta, Winn Parish, Louisiana, and was buried Jun 1910 in Bethlehem Church, Winn Parish, Louisiana. William (Jess) "Bill" Phillips Sr. and Francis Peats beget 9 children:

> General Lee "Dad" Phillips (Twin), ("wild", "horse", "meadow"), born 4 Jan 1875 in Atlanta, Winn Parish, Louisiana; died August 12, 1962 in Atlanta, Winn Parish, Louisiana; buried August 18, 1962 in Bethlehem B. C., Winn Parish, Louisiana. On Jan 9, 1896 in Winn Parish, Louisiana he married Luesaser Sis. Rodgers, (A derivative and meaning "eternal, abiding") born 1878 in, Louisiana; died in Winn Parish, Atlanta, Louisiana; buried in Bethlehem Cem., Atlanta, Louisiana.

> Eliza "Liza" Phillips (Twin), (<u>Named after her paternal grandmother</u>), Eliza, which is a short form of ELIZABETH, and meaning "my God is abundance"). Eliza was the "twin" to her brother General Lee. The twins were born January 4, 1875 in Atlanta, Winn Parish, Louisiana. Prior to her marriage to Tom Wilson, Eliza and Steve Jackson beget a daughter, Ernestine Jackson, born October 7, 1896. On February 6, 1903, in Winn Parish, Louisiana, Eliza married Tom Wilson, born in Atlanta, Winn Parish, Louisiana; He died June 17, 1953, in Cullen, Webster Parish, Louisiana and is buried in Bethlehem B. C., Winn Parish, Louisiana. Tom was the son of Sallie and Henry Wilson (both, previously mentioned).

> Isabella "Isa" Phillips, ("my God is abundance"), born about May 1, 1881 in Atlanta, Ward #6, Winn Parish,

Louisiana; died in Atlanta, Winn Parish, Louisiana; buried in Bethlehem B. C., Winn Parish, Louisiana. She married (1) in Louisiana, Gilbert Mosley (Divorced) ("bright pledge"); (2) Sam Willis. ("God has heard").

Arlevia "Levia" Phillips, ("attached"), born Jul 1882 in Atlanta, Winn Parish, Louisiana; died in California; buried in California. She married/divorced (1) Gilbert L. Mosley ("bright pledge") on February 7, 1901, in Winn Parish, Louisiana. Arlevia then married (2) Albert Starks ("noble" and "bright").

Emanuel "Sam" Phillips, ("God is with us") born about July 1, 1888 in Atlanta, Winn Parish, Louisiana; died about 1964 in Lecompte, Rapides Parish, Louisiana; buried in Lecompte, Rapides Parish, Louisiana. He married/divorced (1) in Louisiana, Rachel Small, (Hebrew name meaning "ewe". In the Old Testament this was the name of the favorite wife of Jacob and the mother of Joseph and Benjamin), born in St. Maurice, Winn Parish, Louisiana; buried in Louisiana, daughter of George Small and Eula Loyd; (2) in Louisiana, Louvenia "Vennie" Green. (While the meaning of her name is unknown, research indicates that it is most probably of Etruscan origin. In Roman legend, a form of the name, Lavinia, was the daughter of King Latinus, the wife of Aeneas, and the ancestor of the Roman people. According to the legend Aeneas named the town of Lavinium in honour of his wife).

Willie (William "Bill") Phillips, Jr. ("will, desire", "helmet, and protection"), born Mar 1889 in Atlanta, Winn Parish, Louisiana; died in Winn Parish, Louisiana; buried in Bethlehem B. C., Winn Parish, Louisiana. He married/divorced (1), Kate Ford, ("pure"), born in Louisiana; (2) in, Louisiana Ina Mae Sneed (Means "mother"), born 10 Feb 1899 in St. Maurice, Winn Parish, Louisiana; died 14 Oct 1993 in Natchitoches, Louisiana; buried 23 Oct 1993 in Old Morning Star, St. Maurice, Louisiana, daughter of Mack "Bill" Sneed and Mary Holmes; (3) in, Louisiana Bertha "Verda" Mathis, ("bright, famous") born in Atlanta, Winn Parish, Louisiana; died in

Atlanta, Winn Parish, Louisiana; buried in Bethlehem B. C., Winn Parish, Louisiana, daughter of Shedrick "Shed" Mathis (Derivative of the name SHADRACH, means "command of Aku" in Akkadian, *Aku* being the name of the Babylonian god of the moon. In the Old Testament Shadrach was the Babylonian name of Hananiah, one of the three men cast into a fiery furnace but saved by God). Note BIOGRAPHY: William's name on his wife's (INA MAE SNEED) funeral program was listed as "Willie Phillips." Napoleon Alexander aka "Coot" Phillips, (This was an old Italian name, used most notably by the French emperor Napoleon Bonaparte (1769-1821), who was born on Corsica. It is possibly derived from the Germanic *Nibelungen,* the name of a race of dwarfs in Germanic legend, which meant "sons of mist"), born 29 Dec 1891 in Atlanta, Winn Parish, Louisiana; died 10 Feb 1981 in Houston, Harris County, Texas; buried 14 Feb 1981 in Bethlehem Church, Winn Parish, Louisiana. On 8 Jun 1916 in Atlanta, Winn Parish, Louisiana, Napoleon married Larcenia "Lar" Fobbs, (A derivative, and means "little fierce one"), born March 17, 1898 in Emden, Winn Parish, Louisiana; christened in Bethlehem Church, Winn Parish, Louisiana; died 4 Jan 1981 in Houston, Harris County, Texas; buried 11 Jan 1981 in Bethlehem Church, Winn Parish, Louisiana. Larcenia was the daughter of Jackson "Jack" Fobbs ("man") and Pauline "Jabie" Veans (Meaning "small" or "humble"). Napoleon and Larcenia beget 12 children; Raymond Phillips advice" and "protector") born 24 Dec 1892 in Atlanta, Winn Parish, Louisiana; died 21 Jun 1982 in Hodge, Jackson Parish, Louisiana; buried 26 June, 1982 in Bethlehem Cem., Atlanta, Louisiana Dorathea Phillips, ("Gift of God") 1920-1980, James Elmore Phillips, ("Holder of the heel", May God provide") 1917 –, Johnnie D Phillips, ("YAHWEH is gracious") 1918 – 2002, Aretha Phillips, ("Virtue") 1923 – , Napoleon R Phillips, Sr. ("Son of mist") 1925 – 1998, Theda Phillips, ("Gift of God") 1927 – , Viriece Marie Phillips, ("Faith", True") April 15, 1933 and died February 1, 2012 in Humble, TX – , Ethel Mae Phillips,

("Noble") 1935 – , Verena Rose Phillips, ("True", "Victory")
1937 – , Lorene Phillips, ("From Laurel") 1938 – Dessarine
(Dess) ("Desirable") February 25, 1929

Raymond Phillips Sr, married (1) in Louisiana, Adline
Harrell, divorced ("noble") born in Louisiana; (2) Viola
Brew, ("violet"), daughter of Henry Brew ("home ruler").
James Elmore Phillips married Elizabeth Louise
Williams, 1927-2012 and they beget Calvin and
Gervasia Larnett

Gervasia married Alvin R. Onezine on August 19,
2006 in Harris County, Texas
Johnnie D Phillips
Aretha Phillips
Napoleon R Sr Phillips married Iva Lee and they beget
Napoleon R. Jr.
Theda Phillips
Viriece Marie Phillips married John Winslow and they
Beget 3 boys and 3 girls: Mildred Winslow was the only
name verified.
Ethel Mae Phillips married Mr. Walker and it is
Unknown how many children they begot
Verena Rose Phillips
Lorene Phillips
Dessarine (Dess) married John "Clyde" (JC) Davis and
they beget Stafford Loys Davis

Lisbon "Shorty" Phillips, (Lisbon is the name of several
places in the world, including a village in Claiborne
Parish, Louisiana. This Louisiana Village of Lisbon is
located east of the parish seat of Homer),born Jul 1897 in
Atlanta, Winn Parish, Louisiana; died 11 Jan 1981 in
Winfield, Winn Parish, Louisiana; Lisbon served as a
Private in the U.S. Army, during WWI, and is buried in
the Alexandria National V.A. Mem. Cemetery, Pineville,
Louisiana. On 17 Jun 1921 in Atlanta, Winn Parish,
Louisiana, he married Mary Fobbs ("my beloved, or "my
love) born 15 Jan 1900 in Emden, Winn Parish,
Louisiana; christened in Bethlehem Church, Winn Parish,
Louisiana; died 27 Sep 1985 in Winnfield Hosp.,

Winnfield, Louisiana; She was buried on 29 Sep 1985 alongside of her late husband at the Alexandria National V.A. Mem. Cemetery, Pineville, Louisiana. Mary was the daughter of Jackson "Jack" Fobbs) and Pauline "Jabie" Veans, (both, previously mentioned).

Laura Phillips, (Feminine form of the Late Latin name *Laurus*, which meant "laurel". This meaning was favorable, since in ancient Rome the leaves of laurel trees were used to create victors' garlands), born 1847 in Charleston County, South Carolina; died 1951 in Louisiana; buried in Bethlehem Church, Winn Parish, Louisiana. She married (1) Mr. Goff, divorced, (2) James McCain.

Edith Phillips ("rich, blessed", and "war"). Her date of birth and date of death are unknown.

The 6 Children begotten of Eliza (Jess) Phillips and Jack Sapp were Louis, Kitty, Benjamin, Eli, Rose Ann, and Elvy/Elvira:

Louis Sapp, ("famous warrior"), born 1864 in Louisiana; died in Louisiana. In 1879, he married Mandy Harris, (previously mentioned), born Dec 1863 in, Louisiana. Louis and Mandy beget 12 children, and they were: Arthur, Annie, Alex, Berry, Kitty, Clemon, Alonzo, Rosann, Jenny, Anna, Mathis, and Elmo

Arthur ("man") was born in 1881. He married Emma/Erma Sneed, who was born in 1888 and died November 4, 1978. Arthur and Emma/Erma beget 6 children; Earl, Jack, Icy B., Mandy, Louonia, and Elie.

Earl ("nobleman", "warrior") was born in 1910, and died March, 1987 in Shreveport, Caddo Parish, LA.

Jack ("Yahweh is gracious") was born January 6, 1912, in Winn, LA., and died February 13, 1961, in Alameda, CA.

Icy B. ("Yahweh is salvation") was born in 1914

Mandy ("lovable, worthy of love"), was born in 1916

Louonia ("silver", "the moon") was born in 1918

Elie ("my God is Yahweh") was born in 11919

Annie ("favor", "grace") was born in 1884

Alex ("defending men", "help") was born in April 18, 1885

Berry ("From the English word referring to the small fruit") was born in 1888

Kitty ("each of the two") was born in 1891

Clemon ("merciful", "gentle') was born in 1895

Alonzo ("noble and ready") was born in November 8, 1897, and died in March, 1978, in Oakdale, Allen, LA.

Rosann ("fame", 'favor", "grace") was born in 1902

Genie ("well born", "good", "well") was born in 1905

Anna ("favor", "grace") was born in 1917

Mathis ("a gift of Yahweh") was born in 1921

Elma ("will", 'desire") was born in 1924

Kitty Sapp (previously mentioned), born 1867 in Louisiana; died in Louisiana. She married in Louisiana Jackson "Jack" Fobbs (previously mentioned), born about 1 Feb 1869 in Natchitoches, Louisiana; died 28 Aug 1966 in , Winn Parish, Louisiana; buried in Bethlehem Cem., Winn Parish, Louisiana, son of Pierre Fobbs (Meaning "stone") and Betsy (Robinson) Robertson ("my God is abundance").

Benjamin Sapp ("son of the south" or "son of the right hand". In the Old Testament, he was the twelfth and youngest son of Jacob and the founder of one of the southern tribes of the Hebrews. He was originally named *(Ben-'oniy)* meaning "son of my sorrow" by his mother Rachel, who died shortly after childbirth, but it was later changed by his father"), was born Mar 1870 in Louisiana; died March 13, 1940, in Winn Parish, Louisiana. On March 5, 1890, in Winn Parish, Ben married Delia Ann Miller ("YAHWEH has drawn"), born about December, 1870, in Louisiana, and they beget 13 children;

Jessie ("gift) born in 1891, Addie ("noble, kind") born in 1892, Edith ("wealth, fortune") born 1894, Hattie ("home, ruler") born 1896, Jenny ("fair, white, smooth") born 1900, Florence ("prosperous, flourishing") born 1901, Mattie ("lady, mistress") born 1904, Grenta ("queen") born 1904, Mildred ("gently, strength") born 1906, Martha ("lady, mistress") 1906, Bennie May ("blessed") born 1906, Harrison ("home, ruler") born 1908, Amelia ("work, rival") born 1910. They also raised grand-daughter, Addie Walker ("noble", "kind") born in 1900 and grand-sons, Milton Walker ("mill town") born in 1920 and Jessie Johnson ("gift") born in 1920.

Eli Sapp, (Means "ascension" or "my God"), born 1873 in Louisiana; died in Louisiana. Eli married Nina Bell (""little girl"), born in 1876, and they beget 9 children; Allen ("handsome"), Clarence ("From the Latin title *Clarensis* which belonged to members of the British royal family. The title ultimately derives from the name of the Clare River in Ireland"), Edward ("rich", "blessed", "guard"), Elizabeth ("my God is abundance"), Dora ("gift of God"), Lee ("meadow"), Eli ("ascension", "my God") Terry ('summer"), and Adger/Edgar ("rich", "blessed").

Rose Ann Sapp, ("fame", "kind", "sort", and "type"),born 1875 in Louisiana; died in Louisiana. She married John Peats Sr. (A derivative, meaning "YAHWEH is gracious") and they beget Allen ("little rock" or "handsome") born in October 1897 and Walter ("ruler of the army") born in July 1899.

Elvy/Elvira Sapp (Meaning "his highness"), born 1877 in Louisiana; died in Louisiana.

My Paternal Line
The Fowler's

FOWLER, a derivative of "bird", and meaning "bird-catcher".

Of My Father's Father's, Father

JOHN FOWLER (Meaning "God is gracious") as documented in the 1850 U.S. Federal Census, Meriwether, Georgia was born about 1820 in South Carolina and was 30 years old at the time of the census. That census also documented HAMPTON FOWLER, believed to be the younger brother of John. (A derivative of the biblical name, Ham, who was one of Noah's three sons and was the ancestor of the Egyptians and Canaanites and means "hot, warm"), as documented in the 1850 U.S. Federal Census was born about 1822 in South Carolina and would have been 28 years old at the time of the census. Hampton was married Hampton was married to Balzora (The Hebrew form of the Akkadian name Bel-sarra-usur meaning "BA'AL protect the king". In the Old Testament Book of Daniel, Belshazzar is the last king of Babylon, who sees the mystical handwriting on the wall, which is interpreted by Daniel to be a sign of the end of the empire), who was 26 years old and born in Georgia about 1824. Hampton and Balzora beget a daughter, Mary A., 4 years old and born in 1846 in Georgia and 2 sons, John, 3 years old, born 1847 in Georgia and a yet un-named newborn, born in 1850 in Georgia. John Fowler was married to Mary (Noted to most likely be an Egyptian name, meaning "beloved", "love"), as documented in the 1850 U.S. Federal Census was born about 1825 in Georgia and was 25 years old. In the 1850 Census, John and Mary was documented as having begotten 2 children; a son, WILLIS FOWLER ("will, desire", "helmet, and as documented in the 1850 U.S. Federal Census was born about protection"), was 2 years old and born in 1848 in Georgia. Willis died in Bienville, LA. While some family members have spelled his name as "Wilas" Fowler, both the 1850 and 1880 U.S. Federal Census documents the spelling as "Willis" and a newborn, yet un-named daughter, born in Georgia.

*I found it quite ironic to note that **as documented in that 1850 U.S. Federal Census** 1. The younger brother, Hampton named his firstborn son, John, after his older brother, 2. He named his first daughter Mary A., after his sister-in-law, and 3. both, Hampton/Balzora and John/Mary had newborn, un-named babies. This irony of the children's names will be further explored in another chapter, entitled NAMES.*

Ten years later, in the 1860 U.S. Federal Census in Tallapoosa, Alabama, Balzora (Now spelled in that census as "Valsora") Fowler was residing in Tallapoosa, Alabama with her now 16 y/o daughter, Mary A., 13 y/o John and 10 y/o Morgan (who was a newborn and un-named in the previous 1850 census in Meriwether, GA., 8 y/o Amanda, 6 y/o Sarah and 3 y/o George H., all born in Georgia. Unfortunately, that census does not indicate a marital status for Balzora and does not list her husband, Hampton. No further records were found to document the lives of John Fowler and his wife, Mary. Given that slavery was not abolished until 1865 (The 13th Amendment was passed by Congress on January 31 and ratified on December 6th), at which time John would have been 45 y/o, Mary would have been 40 y/o and Hampton would have been 43 y/o, while they may have very well survived slavery, like so many, perhaps they were unable to endure the tedious journey from South Carolina to Louisiana or settled in a different area.

*There remains some speculation as to whether the link between the previously noted members are indeed "true"

The next documented information located y years post the passage of the 13th Amendment is the 1870 U.S. Federal Census, Bienville, Bienville Parish, Louisiana, notes the family of Margaret Clark ("Pearl"), who later married Willis Fowler. Born in 1856 in Georgia, Margaret was the 3rd eldest daughter of Phillip ("Friend", "lover") and Rosetta Clark ("Fame", "kind"), born in 1827 in Georgia. Phillip, born in 1820 in Georgia was the son of Charlot Clark ("man"), born in 1795 in Alabama. As of the 1870 Census, Phillip and Rosetta beget 7 children; Bell ("My God is an oath"), born 1847 in Georgia, Jane ("YAHWEH is gracious"), born 1852 in Georgia, Margaret ("Pearl"), born 1856 in Georgia. Between 1856 and 1860, the family moved to Bienville, Louisiana, as James ("May God protect"), born 1860 was born in Louisiana, Lizzy ("My God is an oath"), born in 1864 in Louisiana, Ann ("Favor", "Great"), born in 1866 in Louisiana and Jonah ("Dove"), born in 1870 in Louisiana. Phillip's mother (Charlot), was also living with them and noted to have been 75 years old and born 1795 in Alabama.

The 1880 U.S. Federal Census find Phillip and Rosetta still residing in Sparta, Bienville Parish, Louisiana and residing with them is daughter, Jane Clark now 30 years old and 6 grandchildren (It is not clear if all/any of the 6 grandchildren are Jane's children. Those 6 are; Lizzy C. ("My God is an oath"), Clark ("Cleric" or "Scribe") 13 y/o, Black, Ann Clark ("Favor" or "Great") 10 y/o, Mulatto, **Josiah Clark** ("YAHWEH supports") 9 y/o, Mulatto, Ely Clark ("Ascension") 7 y/o, Black, Rosetta Clark ("Fame", "Kind") 3 y/o and Lucy Jane Clark ("Light"), 1 y/o, Mulatto.

NOTE: at some point**, Josiah Clark changed his name to Joseph Samuel Clark.** He attended public and private school in Sparta, Louisiana, went on to received his B. A. from Leland College in 1901 and an M. A. Degree from Selma University in 1913. He did post graduate work at Harvard and Chicago Universities.

Dr. Joseph Samuel Clark
Clark, Joseph S. [Samuel], b. 1871 d. 1944

Dr. Clark, an outstanding citizen in the Baton Rouge African American community, presided over Baton Rouge College and the Louisiana Colored Teachers Association. The Louisiana Constitutional Convention of 1921 authorized the reorganization and expansion of Southern University; and Legislative Act 100 of 1922, provided that the institution be reorganized under the control of the State Board of Education. Clark presided over Southern University during a period of transition for the institution. The student enrollment grew from forty-seven students to 500 students and many of the school's early buildings were built during this time. Clark presided until his retirement in 1938, at which time the position was given to **his son, Dr. Felton Grandison Clark** ("Undefined"), **a renowned speaker and gentleman**.

Dr. Felton Grandison Clark
Clark, Felton G. [Grandison], b. 1903 d. 1970

Under Dr. Joseph Samuel Clark's tenure, the university underwent tremendous growth. About 33 of 114 current buildings were erected in his 30 years at the university. The student enrollment grew from 500 to nearly 10,000 students. Due to the reluctance of LSU Law School to admit African Americans into its law program and a law suit that was filed, a special Louisiana Convention allowed a law program, the Southern University Law Center to come to Southern University in 1947. The university was one of the first historically black colleges to receive a visit from a First Lady, Eleanor Roosevelt, in 1943. Also during Clark's tenure, Southern University at New Orleans (SUNO) (1956) and Southern University at Shreveport/Bossier City (SUSLA) (1964) were founded. They were later incorporated into the Southern University System in 1974. Dr. Clark served as president of Southern University in Baton Rouge from 1913 to 1938. He was also the president of the National Association of Teachers in Colored Schools in 1916 and superintendent of the Louisiana State School for Negro Blind.

Dr. Clark retired in 1938 and died in 1944, in New Orleans and is buried on the grounds of Southern University in Scotlandville. He, his wife and son are buried on campus in 3 above ground tombs.

The 1880 U.S. Federal Census, notes **Willis**, still residing in Bienville, Louisiana, 31 years old (Records to document the date/location of his death were not located) and married to previously noted, Margaret A. Clark, 24 years old. At the time of the 1880 census, Willis and Margaret A. had 3 sons, Frank, John Henry and Henry and 2 daughters, Caroline and Mattie. Willis and Margaret A. went on to beget 7 additional children (for a total of 12); George, Laura, Colzee, Augusta, Charlie, Walter and Joe.

John H. ("God is gracious"), was born about 1874 in Heflin, LA, and died on July 16, 1952 in Fryberg, Bienville, LA. John married Lucy Wallace ("light"). Lucy was the daughter of Irvin AKA Irving Wallace and Tamar AKA Tania, was born in Oct. 1877 in Bienville, LA and died in Bienville, LA. John and Lucy beget 8 children; Theodore Henderson, Atkin Thomas, Johnnie, Ida Mae, Pirleaner, Irene, Gradie, and Anner Lou.

Theodore ("gift of God") was born Feb 15, 1914 Bienville, LA., and died Sep 12, 1997 in Pontiac, MI. He married Mamie Bessie Wilson ("wished for child") and they beget 4 children; Charles James (Twin) ("man", "army", warrior"), Churley Gene (Twin) (meaning "bright clearing"), Betty Gene ("my God is abundance"), and Jurlean ("rule of the spear", "soft", and "tender").

Their progeny were previously mentioned.

Atkin T. ("fire"), was born Sept 16, 1905 in Bienville, LA., and died Feb 1, 1985 in Los Angeles, CA. Atkins married (1). Ruby Lee Nolen Fowler and they beget 3 children; Theresa ("summer"), Booker T. ("maker of books"), and Inez Valaida Fowler ("chaste", "lamb"). He then married (2) Cleola Hamilton (Means "crown of laurel"), born March 25, 1915, in Palestine, TX. to Wade Hamilton, Sr. ("to go"), and Lucy Ann (Brooks) Hamilton ("light").

Theresa, born June 13, 1935, married/divorced Robert McNair, Sr. and they beget 1 son, Robert, Jr. and 1 daughter, June

June ("The name of the month") was born May 8, 1955
Robert, Jr. ("bright fame") was born May 4, 1958 and beget 1 son, Justin and 1 daughter, Robyn

Justin ("just") was born November 22, 1988
Robyn ("bright fame") was born August 13, 1994

Booker T. ("maker of books"), born December 2, 1932 in Heflin, Louisiana, married Willia B. Griffin aka Billie ("will", "desire") and they beget 1 daughter, Bridgett Fowler

Bridgett ("exalted one") was born November 13, 1965, and married/divorced Gabriel Garcia ("strong man of God"). They beget 1 daughter, Brianne and 1 son, Garrett

Brianne ("hill", "high", "noble"), born October 15, 1991
Garrett ("rule of the spear"), born August 17, 1993

Inez Valaida Fowler, born March 24, 1937 and died February 12, 1991 in St. Paul, Minnesota, beget 1 son, Terry Fowler

Johnnie ("Yahweh is gracious"), was born April 15, 1921 in Bienville, LA., and died Feb. 11, 2003 in Toledo, OH. He married Canary Ward ("God gave"), born April 10, 1924, and died April 7, 1995. Johnny and Canary beget 9 children; Valerie Jean, O'Donald, Sandra, Kenneth, John Michael, Sharon, Leonard, Vivian, and Carmen.

Valerie Jean ("to be strong") aka Nazaarah, married Mansour Sei'fullah Bey (Lawrence Marvin Barnes, Sr.) ("victorious"), and they beget and blended their family with, Lawrence Jr. (victorious"), Christopher ((Meaning "bearing Christ", derived from *(Christos)* combined with *(phero)* "to bear, or to carry"), Taleb ("royal fortress"), Joshua ("Yahweh is salvation"), David ("beloved"), and Marvin Mezzavilla ("marrow famous");

Grandchildren Rashard Barnes ("brave power"), Kaleb Ann (Means "dog" in Hebrew. In the Old Testament this was the name of one of the twelve spies sent by Moses into Israel), Niko ("victory"), Josiana ("he will add"), Joshua II ("Yahweh is salvation"), and Patience Bey ("to suffer").

Lawrence, Jr. ("victorious") married Chesetta ("pure").

Kim ("royal fortress"), married Christopher Schoolcraft (Meaning "bearing Christ", derived from *(Christos)* combined with *(phero)* "to bear, or to carry").

Taleb ("seeker of knowledge") married Kimberly ("royal fortress")

Joshua ("Yahweh is salvation") married Niesha ("night")

David ("beloved") Mezzavilla

Marvin ("marrow famous") Mezzavilla

O'Donald ("lion of God"), beget one daughter, LaShanda Yvette ("good spear").

She married Akorli Nukunya (Nigerian name, meaning "One who is strong, in spite of being small"). LaShanda and Akorli beget 2 daughters; Catrice ("pure") and Seli ("altar", "rock")

Catrice, born in 1988 married Antwan Owns and They beget 2 sons, James ("holder of the heel", or "supplanter") and Aiden ("fire")

Sandra Lee ("to defend", "help"), born September 9, 1949. On August 19, 1978, she married William Gerald Hutcheson("will, desire", "helmet, and protection"), born September 1, 1948, and they beget one son, William, Jr. ("will, desire", "helmet, and protection")and daughter, Shannon.

Shannon E.
William, Jr., born

Kenneth ("handsome")

John Michael (Yahweh is gracious"), beget Maya Bell, Nannie and Joshua

> Maya Bell ("A derivative of Mary, meaning, "my beloved" or "*my* love"), born August 26, 1974. Maya and Prentis Hubbard ("first formed") beget Christian ("anointed"), born September 5, 1994, Jacob ("holder of the heel", "supplanter"), born July 23, 2006, Gabrielle ("strong man of God")born January 20, 2009 and Taviahn Atlas Fowler ("twin")
> Joshua (previously mentioned) beget 1 daughter, Alissa ("against")

Sharon, ("From an Old Testament place name meaning "plain"), beget Angela. Sharon married/divorced Jack Mabrey ("Yahweh is gracious"), and they beget Kamilah ("perfection") and, born March 14, ("queen").

> Angela ("messenger") beget 1son, Terrell Hawkins ("to pull", "stubborn"), and 3 daughters; Alayia Clemons (high", "lofty"), Akalah Clemons ("intelligent"), and Amond Clemons ("the hidden one").
>> Terrel beget 1 son, T.J. Hawkins ("to pull", "stubborn").
> Kamilah beget 1 son, Kyle Dread
> Malikah born March 3, married Leonard Horton and they beget 1 son, Leonard Jr.

Leonard ("brave lion"), born Aug 13, 1956, married Elysa Davis ("noble", "kind"), and they beget Tanela ("all sweetness"), Everett ("brave", "hardy") and Devan ("fawn", "stag", "ox").

> Tanela married Andrae Hicks ("man"), and they beget Ashton Tavon Hicks (derived from a place name which meant "ash tree town" in Old English) Amond ("the hidden one") and 1 daughter, Aubrey Talynn ("Power") born Wednesday, February 11, 2015, Ohio (8Lbs, 10 oz, 22 inches).

Vivian ("alive") and Bryant Coleman ("hill", or "high noble"), beget daughters, Alyssa ("noble", "king"), born April 17, 1979, Constance ("constant", "steadfast"), born July 20, 1981, Essence ("to be") and 1 son, Austin ("great", "to increase"). Vivian also beget son, Skyler Walker ("scholar") and daughters, Darlene Walker ("From the English word "darling", "beloved". This name has been in use since the beginning of the 20th century") and Christina Walker ("anointed").

Alyssa beget Keara ("clear, bright. Famous") born January 7, 2000, Kiara ("clear, bright. Famous") and 2 sons, Dawane ("shine", "sky") born April 23, 2002 and Daveon ("fawn"), born April 23, 2004

Constance beget Salina ("moon"), Kenyi ("innocent") and Niamiaha ("comforted by YAHWEH")

Austin beget 4 daughters, Adrea ("of a man"), Aunndrea ("of a man"), Jesenia ("from Jessenia – a type of palm tree native to the Amazonia, that produces edible fruits rich in high quality oil") and Calena ("moon")

Skyler beget Skyler Walker, Jr. ("scholar") and an unborn son, due January, 2015.

Carmen Denise ("song") was born July 28, 1962 in Toledo, Ohio and died August 8, 2006, in Toledo, OH. Carmen and Cedric Johnson, Sr.* ("first formed") beget a daughter, Alexis Breann Johnson ("to defend", "help"), born March 9, 1998 in Toledo, OH and a son, Adrian Johnson ("first formed").

*Cedric passed away just 6 years after Carmen, on March 2, 2012, as a result of a prolonged cardiac illness, leaving their minor children, Alexis and Adrian, in the care of and to be raised by his family, in Toledo, Ohio.

Ida Mae ("work", "labor"), was born May 2, 1909 in Bienville, LA., and died July 1, 2006, Ringgold, Bienville, LA. Ida Mae married John T. Smith (Yahweh is gracious"), and they beget 9 children; Bertha, Mattie, Bessye, Ruby, Rutherine, Wallace, Thomas, Robert aka Bob and Henry aka Sonny.

Bertha ("bright" "famous")

Mattie ("strength in battle")

Bessye (my God is abundance") married Robert Smith, born April 2, 1956. Bessye begot a son, Damion Harold Edwards. She and Robert beget daughter, Dedri Charrie ("ruler of the people") and son, Jamaal Smith ("beauty").

Dedri Charrie married Alonzo Wilhike and they beget Dolores ("sorrow") and Brandeis ("burnt wine", "brandy").

Ruby (Simply means "ruby" from the name of the precious stone)

Rutherine ("friend"),

Wallace ("Welsh", "foreigner")

Thomas ("twin")

Robert ("bright fame")

Henry ("home ruler")

Pirleaner ("from the gemstone "pearl" that imparts health and wealth"), was born December 26, 1912 in Bienville, LA., and died March 20, 2007 in Heflin, Webster Parish, LA. She married Jepp Evans ("peace"), and they beget through adoption, one daughter, Allie Mae.

Allie Mae ("noble")

Irene ("peace") was born June 26. 1919, Bienville, LA., died October 26, 2000, in Houston, TX. She married (1) Walter Jackson ("ruler of the army"), (2) Curtis Dean. Irene had no children.

Grady ("noble"), was born in January 19, 1907 in Bienville, LA., died February 20, 1987 in Bellwood, Cook County, IL. She married Felmo Harvey ("ever good"), and they beget 3 children; Mary Lue, Willie James, and Arthur Ray.

Mary Lue ("beloved", "love") was born in 1935, beget 1 son, Eddie Joe Harvey, born "May 13, 1956 in Harris County, Texas and 1daughter, Patricia Adams, born in Cook County, Illinois

Willie James ("will, desire", "helmet, and protection") was born in 1932 and died in 2003. He married Earnestine and they beget 1 daughter, Kim and 2 sons, Joseph and Darrell

Arthur Ray ("bear", "man"), was born in 1939

Anner Lou ("favor" and "grace'), was born April 30, 1910, died November 7, 2007 in Shreveport, Caddo parish, LA. She married Caldwell, Sr. ("heart", "mind" "spirit"), born October 9, 1914 and died January 21, 1963. Anner Lou and Hudson, Sr. beget 6 children; Mary Helen, Hudson, Jr., John T., Roosevelt, Walter and Irene.

Mary Helen, ("beloved", "love") born in 1940, and died December 27, 1997. She married Leon Craig ("lion").

Hudson, Jr., aka Hearter, ("heart", "mind" "spirit") born in 1942.

Hudson beget 2 daughters, Ebonie, Lamonda and 2 sons, Claude and Chris Harrison.

Ebonie ("From the English word *ebony* for the black wood which comes from the ebony tree."), born in Chicago, IL., 1978, beget one daughter, Anna Brooklyn Caldwell-Sims ("favor", or "grace"), born July 20, 2009. Lamonda ("little light") born in Chicago, IL.1986, beget one daughter, London Ann Scott ("From the name of the capital city of the United Kingdom, the meaning of which is uncertain."), born June 17, 2009.

Claude ("From a Roman family name which was derived from Latin *claudus* meaning "lame, crippled". This was the family name of several Roman emperors of the 1st century, including the emperor known simply as Claudius. He was poisoned by his wife Agrippina in order to bring her son Nero (Claudius's stepson) to power.") was born in Chicago, IL.

Chris Harrison was born in Chicago, IL

John. ("Yahweh is gracious") born March 3, 1945. He married (1) Carol Wilson ("song", or "hymn"), born February 26, 1946 and they beget one daughter, Gabriella. Carol died April 16, 1976, in Chapel Hill, NC. On November 6, 1982 John married (2) Valerie Climons ("to be strong") in Chicago, Il, and they beget Jamal.

Gabriella/Gabby ("strong man of God") born June 30, 1972. On August 5, 1995, she married Aamon R. Miller ("the hidden one") in Chicago, IL. They beget 2 daughters, Carolyn ("song" or "hymn"), born March 24, 1997 in Chicago, IL. and Camryn ("nose"), born March 13, 1999, in Chicago, IL.
Jamal ("beauty") born February 26, 1985, beget one daughter, Taylor Olivia, ("to cut") born July 8, 2006, in VA.

Roosevelt ("rose field") born October 9, 1946, Shreveport, LA. on May 31, 1969, he married Brenda Ann Weathers ("sword") and they beget three sons, Damian Rachard, Anthony Troy, and Brandon

Damian R. ("to tame") was born June 17, 1975, in Flint, MI. He married Dinita Inez Mack ("God is my judge"), born May 3, 1979 in Oklahoma City, OK. and they beget 2 sons, Dayne ("valley") Rachard, Dayce Roosevelt ("A variant of Dayne, meaning Vally") and twins, a boy, Dean Royce("Valley") and a girl, Danae Inez (("In Greek Danaë was the princess of Argos and the mother of Perseus by Zeus, who came to her in the form of a shower of gold")born April 9, 2015.

> Dayne was born March 311. 2008 in Austin, TX
> Dayce was born October 19, 2010in Austin, TX
> Baby Boy, Dean born April 9, 2015 in Austin, TX. 6lbs 3 oz, 19 inches
> Baby Girl, Danae Inez born 1 minute after her brother, April 9, 2015 in Austin, TX. 4 lbs 3 oz, 18 inches

> Anthony T. ("English form of the Roman family name *Antonius*, which is of unknown Etruscan origin. The most notable member of the Roman family was the general Marcus Antonius (called Mark Antony in English), who for a period in the 1st century ruled the Roman Empire jointly with Augustus.") born December 20, 1970. He married Heather McGarry ("From the English word *heather* for the variety of small shrubs with pink or white flowers which commonly grow in rocky areas") and they beget one son, Reece Caldwell ("enthusiasm")

> Reece was born May 13, 2003, in MI.

Brandon ("prince") born November 25, 1984 in Flint, MI., died February 12, 2007, in Flint, MI.

Walter ("ruler of the army") born June 10, 1949 in Shreveport, LA. On August 14, 1971, he married Linda Harris ("soft", "tender"). They beget 2 daughters, Portia and Joy.

> Portia ("offering") born in 1975 in California, married/divorced Jacobi Thompson, ("holder of the heel", "supplanter") born in 1975, and they beget Codi

("son of wealth/fortune") born in 2007, and Jacobi Bernard, II ("holder of the heel" or supplanter") born in 2009.

Joy ("delight", "great pleasure") born 1978, in California, beget Dejah Pop ("already seen"), born in 2003.

Irene ("peace") was born June 27, 1953 in Shreveport, LA., and died in 1978 in Shreveport, LA.

Caroline ("army" and "warrior"), was born July 1873 in Bienville, LA. She beget 4 children, Cleveland, Anna, Early, and Willie

Cleveland ("hilly land') was born in 1894

Anna ("favor", "grace") was born in 1895 Early ("nobleman, warrior") was born January 2, 1898, and died February, 1984 in Coushatta, Red River, LA. He married Savannah ("open plain, field", from the English word for the large grassy plain, ultimately deriving from the Native American word *zabana*"), and they beget 12 children; Frank, Lizzie, Carline, Butt, Bill, Anna, Johnny Ruth, Earline, Pauline, Matlean, Charles H., and Willie. By 1930, Early and Savannah were living in De Bastrop, Ashley County, Arkansas

Frank ("Frenchman")
Lizzie ("my God is abundance")
Carline ("army", "warrior")
Butt ("friend")
Bill ("will, desire", "helmet, and protection")
Annie Ruth ("favor", "grace")
Johnny Ruth ("Yahweh is gracious")
Earline ("nobleman", "warrior")
Pauline ("small", "humble")
Matlean ("tower")

Charles Henry ("man"), born March 30, 1925 in Webster Parish, Louisiana. He married Valarie Ann Carnish, ("to be strong"), born February 19, 1952 and they beget 3 daughters; Loretta Ann, Loneicia Pauline and Lorrina Shellaine

Loretta Ann (From the Old French form of the Occitan name *Aliénor*. It was first borne by the influential Eleanor of Aquitaine (12th century), who was the queen of Louis VII, the king of France, and later Henry II, the king of England), born October 7, 1967 and married Rodney Moore ("fame")

Loneicia Pauline ("tower"), born in 1970 and beget a son, Major P. Fowler

Major was born in 1985

Lorrina Shellaine ("From the name of a region in France, originally meaning "kingdom of LOTHAR". Lothar was a Frankish king, the great-grandson of Charlemagne), born in 1972

Willie ("will, desire", "helmet, and protection") married Freda Mae Young ("counsel", "fair", "peace"), and they beget one son, William("will, desire", "helmet, and protection").

Annie Ruth married 1. Albert Loud, 2. Eugene Lipkins. Annie Ruth and Albert beget 7 children; Betty, Albert Joe Sr., Johnny Wayne., Eugene, Debra Ann, Bruce, and Sylvia Damiece

Betty ("my God is abundance") born September 11, 1952, and beget 2 children; Yolonda ("violet"), and Corey Dejuan ("horn").

Yolonda was born 1969, she married Carlos Garza ("man") and they beget Christopher Corey and Brianna Destiny

Christopher ("bearing Christ") was born in 1995

Brianna ("hill", "high", "noble")

Albert Sr. ("noble", "bright") beget 3 children; Albert, Jr., ("noble", "bright"), Diamond ("invincible", "untamed"), and Mattie ("strength in battle").

Johnny W. "Yahweh is gracious"

Eugene ("well born")

Debra Ann ("bee")

Bruce ("From a Scottish surname, of Norman origin, which probably originally referred to the town of Brix in France.

Sylvia ("wood", "forest")

Pauline was born in February 11, 1938 in Heflin, LA., married (1) Theo Coleman ("gift of God"), born April 24, 1935 and died February 2001. (2) Eugene Brooks ("well born"), born November 27, 1936 in Edna, TX; Pauline and Theo beget 3 children; Linda, Olester E., and Glynis.

Linda, born November 14, 1955 ("soft", "tender") in Shreveport, LA. Linda married Loren Watts and beget Lachelcia Kewanna Watts, (Derivative meaning "lily") born November 16, 1979, in Houston, TX.

Lachelcia and Frederick Smith beget Karsyn Bailey Smith (means "child of carr", meaning a landform, wetland, a fen overgrown with trees, The name originated as an English name) born July 22, 2010.

Olester Earl (meaning "to camp", "dweller by the wild olive tree"), born January 9, 1958 in Shreveport, LA.

Glynis born ("pure, clean, holy", born October 22, 1963 in Houston, TX.

Frank ("Frenchman") was born in January, 1874 in Dublin, LA. and died July 8, 1918 in Palmer, Ellis County, Texas.
Mattie ("Gift of Yahweh") was born in 1878 in Bienville, LA.
Henry ("foreign")was born in 1880 in Bienville, LA.
George ("earth" and "work") was born in 1883 in Bienville, LA.
Laura ("laurel") was born in 1885 in Bienville, LA.
Colzee ("fierce") was born in 1886 in Bienville, LA.
Augusta ("great", "venerable", "to increase") was born in 1887 in Bienville, LA.
Charlie ("man", "army", "warrior") was born in 1888 in Bienville, LA. Charlie married Dosia Johnson, (Latinized and feminine form of the Greek name, Theodosius, meaning "giving to God"), daughter of James Johnson ("holder of the heel" or "supplanter") and Sabina Dean (the original Welsh name of the River Severn. It was the name of a princess who

was drowned in the Severn meaning "sabine woman"), born 1896 and died in 1986. Charlie and Dosia beget 8 children; Beatrice, Margaret, Pete, Charlie, Jr., Willie, Joe, Odessa and Leroy

Beatrice ("voyager", "traveler")

Margaret ("pearl")

Pete ("stone")

Charlie, Jr. ("man") was born August 27, 1917 and died May 29, 1999, in North Chicago, IL. Charlie, Jr. married Erma Lee Walker ("whole", "universal"), and they beget Shirley, Ramona Marie and

Charles Anthony.

Shirley (Meaning "**bright clearing**"), married Minister Charles J. Ivy (" man", "army", "warrior") and they beget Cedric, born March 12, 1985 in North Chicago, IL and Alicia, (Latinized form of Alice and the French form, Aalis and Adelaide, meaning "noble, kind") born November 1, 1987 in North Chicago, IL.

Cedric (Invented by an author in 1819, based on the name "Cerdic"; the name of the founder of the kingdom of Wessex in the 6th century), married Anissa (A combination of Anna and the suffix *issa*, meaning ("Favor or Grace") and they beget a daughter, Ryiah Gabrielle, born September 15, 2013 in Waukegan, IL.

Ramona (Mona), (The feminine form of Ramon and the Spanish form of Raymond, meaning 'advice and protector") born 1963 in North Chicago, IL. Ramona married Brian Lundy, Sr. ("Hill, high, noble") and they beget Brian Keith, Jr. and Joslyn.

Joslyn (A variant of *Jocelyn*, derived from the name of the German tribe, the Gauts) was born in 1983

Brian, Jr. ("Hill, high, noble") was born in 1986 and as a decorated and beloved USA Navy Medic died in military service to his country on September 9, 2011, in Afghanistan.

Willie ("will", "desire", "helmet and protection") born in 1899, married Freda Mae Young and they beget 1 son, William

Joe ("he will add")

Odessa (Meaning "myrtle tree" or "to hate" in Hebrew. In the Old Testament this was the Hebrew name of Queen Esther).

Leroy ("the king") was born 1931 in Arkansas. He married Otha Logwood, (Possible feminine derivative of the Hebrew name, Ohad, meaning "united") born August 6,1932 in Monroe, LA. They beget 2 daughters, Kathy ("pure") and Andrea ("of a man")

Kathy born September 28, 1961 in Berkley, CA. She married Mr. Thornton and they beget 3 children; Porsche ("short", "wolf"), Joie ("he will add") and Andre ("man")

Porsche was born October 3, 1983 in Oakland, CA. She beget 2 sons, Dewayne Ramsey ("dark") and Pierston Thornton-Price ("priest town")

Dewayne Ramsey, born January 2, 1999 in Hayward, California

Pierston Thornton-price born January 26, 2007 in Atlanta, Georgia

Joie was born July 14, 1990 in Haywood, CA.

Andre was born January 10, 1995 in Oakland, CA.

Andrea ("of a man") married Anthony Davis ("English form of the Roman family name *Antonius*, which is of unknown Etruscan origin. The most notable member of the Roman family was the general Marcus Antonius (called Mark Antony in English), who for a period in the 1st century BC ruled the Roman Empire jointly with Augustus. When their relationship turned sour, he and his mistress Cleopatra were attacked and forced to commit suicide, as related in Shakespeare's tragedy 'Antony and Cleopatra' (1606)) and they beget 1 daughter, Andreca ("of a man") born June 26, 1994 and 1 son, Anthony, Jr. ("English form of the Roman family name *Antonius*, which is of unknown Etruscan origin.

Walter ("ruler of the army") was born in 1889 in Bienville, LA.

Joe ("he will do") was born in 1890 in Bienville, LA.

My Paternal Line
The Wallace's
WALLACE, meaning "Welsh" or "foreigner"

Of My Father's Mother, Lucy Wallace

Irvin aka Irving W. Wallace ("boar" and "friend") was born in June 1852, Shelby County, Alabama, and died in Louisiana. While I could not locate any documents of his death, it is noted that by the 1910 Census, his wife is documented as a widow, so we can estimate his death between 1900, when he was 47 y/o and 1910. According to the 1900 U.S. Federal Census, it is documented that Irvin's father was born in North Carolina and his mother was born in Georgia. Irvin and Tamar aka Tama Tillman ("Means "palm tree" in Hebrew. Tamar was the daughter-in-law of Judah in the Old Testament") were married January 2, 1874 in Webster Parish, Louisiana, when he was 22 y/o and she was 23 y/o. Tamar was born July 1851 in Louisiana and died in Louisiana. According to the 1910 U.S. Federal Census, it is documented that Tamar's father was born in North Carolina and her mother was born in South Carolina. Irvin and Tamar beget 5 children; Lucy, Duncan M., Carrie, Mary Jane, and Tillman W.

> Lucy ("light") married John Fowler (previously mentioned), and their progeny were previously mentioned. Lucy was born in Oct. 1877 in Bienville, LA and died in Bienville, LA. John and Lucy beget 8 children; Theodore Henderson, Atkin Thomas, Johnny, Ida Mae, Pirleaner, Irene, Gradie, and Anner Lou.

Duncan M. ("brown warrior") was born February, 1880 in Bienville, LA. He married Josephine ("he will add"), and they beget 2 children, Eddie and Verda.

      Eddie ("rich", "blessed", "guard") was born in 1907

      Verda ("rose") was born in 1910

Carrie B. ("warrior") was born July 1882 in Louisiana. She beget 5 children, Josephine, Irvin, Tillman, Tessie, and Helen.

      Josephine ("he will add") was born in 1903 in Louisiana

      Irvin was born in 1908 and died in 1967

      Tessie was born in 1910

      Tillman, Jr. ("people") was born January 17, 1912 in Louisiana. The 1920 Census records documents Tillman at the age of 7 y/o, living with his adult cousins, Frank and Angeline Walker in Dubberly, Webster Parish, LA. Social Security Records indicate that he died December 13, 2000, in Dubberly. Tillman married Mary Gray and they beget 6 children; Dora, Odella, Tommy Lee, Eugene, and Roosevelt and Ervin. According to the 1940 U.S. Federal Census, Webster Parish, LA., Tillman was now married to Fannie Mae Shepherd, born in 1916 and they beget Willie Edward Wallace

            Tommy Sr. married Fannie M. and they beget Tommy Lee, Jr., Creighton Dejuan, Carlos T., Carmonice Evash, Cher LaDina and Carrie Joanna

                  Tommy, Jr. married on June 30, 2001,1. Geisha Kennette Wallace, born in Louisiana, and they beget daughter, Excellence. Tommy and Geisha divorced October 15, 2010. 2. He married Shantell Washington and they beget Ali.

                  Carrie, named after her great grandmother, married Mr. Smith

                  Carlos and Lakeshia West beget Carldarius T.

Tessie ("summer") was born in 1910 in Louisiana.

Helen ("torch") was born in 1916 in Louisiana.

Roosevelt was born in 1934

Ervin was born in 1936

Willie Edward was born in 1939

Mary Jane ("YAHWEH is gracious") was born December, 1873 in Dubberly, Louisiana and died January 6, 1946,in Shreveport, Caddo Parish, Louisiana. In 1896, Mary J. married Joseph L. Johnson ("he will add") was born in 1874 in Louisiana and according to the 1900 Federal Census, Webster Parish, Louisiana, but by the 1910 Census, Mary Jane was listed as widowed. Joseph and Mary J. beget 1 son, Joseph Webster (Buddy), and 4 daughters; Gertrude, Eunice, Josey and Elizabeth

Gertrude was born about 1898 in Louisiana.

Elizabeth ("my God is an oath", "my God is abundance") was born 1899

Eunice ("good victory") was born in 1902

Josey ("he will add") was born in 1903

Joseph Webster aka Buddy (means "weaver") was born in 1905

Beyond the 1900 Federal Census no additional documents were located for Joseph, Jane or their children.

Tillman Webster Wallace ("people") was born July 3, 1888 in Webster Parish, LA and died July 19, 1978, in Chicago, Cook County, IL. In 1911, Tillman married Rebecca Jane Gipson, born in 1892 (Meaning "a snare". This was the name of the wife of Isaac and the mother of Esau and Jacob in the Old Testament), and died in 1948. I located 2 US Draft Cards for Tillman; one dated June 5, 1917, in Allen County, LA. On that card, Tillman lived in Oakdale, LA., lists his employer as Bowman Hicks Lumber Co., states he is married with 3 children. According to his 1942 US World War II Draft Registration Card, Tillman was employed by the Louisiana Central Lumber Co., in Clarks, LA., he was 5'10", weighed 158 lbs. and his left eye was missing. Tillman and Rebecca beget 3 children, Irvin, Garland, and William

Irvin ("boar" and "friend") was born in 1909

Garland ("triangle land") was born in 1913
William ("will", "desire", "helmet and protection") was
born in 1915

Unfortunately, it proved a challenge locating documents of the Wallace segment of our family tree. While it was indeed a test, I am however, not deterred or otherwise discouraged, but prayerful that after the publication of this edition, one of my relatives will take up the mantle and publish a revised edition, to include the addition of hundreds more Wallace's.

Missing But Certainly Not Forgotten

As expected, but yet unfortunately, many census records, family records and/or simple broken connections presented an impossible hurdle to allow me to include each and every family member in this book.

Nevertheless, in loving memory and acknowledgement of those family members who were not discovered, included or mentioned, I dedicate this page to them, for truly, though their names may be missing, they shall never, ever, be forgotten.

Our Human Spirit

As I prepare to complete this work, more so now, than I believe ever before, I am truly astonished by the human spirit. For all that we endure, so many things we have witnessed, for the endless trials and strife, the countless successes and defeats, the sorrows and joys, the losses and wins, somehow that unfathomable spirit that obviously only the Lord could have built within us, makes allowances for us to get pass, go beyond, move ahead and even overcome so much of our experiences and simply proceed through this life. While a good number find use of unfortunate crutches to limp their way in the course of the process, most, I believe, find a way to call upon that spirit, deep within to help them make it to the end. When I think about personal experiences of some close family members and even some of my own, I am simply baffled on one hand and yet, pleasantly amazed on the other. The resilience of our human spirit is surely, most impossible something that we do not project on our own accord, but has to be, most assuredly by and through the mighty hand of God.

This work of exploring, seeking, finding and documenting my ancestors have afforded me the privilege to examine some lives from the moment of their birth, throughout the time of their life and onward to their death and what I can confirm to any who dare read of the accounts and genealogies herein, truly it has been the hand of God who has and continues to cover and rests upon the generations of my maternal, Wilson-Jess/Phillips and my paternal, Fowler-Wallace Family. An unyielding spirit of destiny and hope. Having confirmed and acknowledged His grace and mercies upon our predecessors, I pray likewise, for us, our children, their children and their future generations. I pray blessings of salvation, love, peace and the strong hand of our Lord and Savior upon our souls and the privilege to simply smile, knowing, that we don't own all the problems in this world.

Loving You, *Jurlean Fowler Avery*

BEGOTTEN
Proudly Presents
Documents of Hope

In Memory of a Hero - Brian Keith Lundy, Jr.

July 29, 1986 – September 9th, 2011

Jurlean Fowler Avery

On Friday, February 24th, 2012 accompanied by my husband, Charles, my eldest niece, Janice A. Rice and my eldest nephew, SgtMaj Mark A. Byrd, Sr.we travelled to Camp Lejeune, N.C. at the invitation of our cousin, Ramona Fowler and her daughter, Joslyn to attend a Memorial Service in honor of Ramona's son, Hospitalman Second Class (FMF SW), Brian K. Lundy, Jr., who sacrificed his life in service to our country on September 9th, 2012 in Afghanistan. It was a true honor to be in the very midst of such love and honor.

For those of you who do not know the family lineage by memory, Ramona Fowler is the second daughter of the late Charles Fowler (Aug 27 1917 - May 29 1999) and Erma Lee Walker Fowler of North Chicago, IL; Charles was the son of the late Charlie Fowler (1888-?) and Dosia Johnson Fowler (1896 – 1986). Charlie was the son of Willis Fowler (1848 - ?) and Margaret A. Fowler (1856 - ?).

Brian joined the United States Navy May 15, 2006 and became a decorated soldier, receiving the Purple Heart (Posthumously), Navy and Marine Corps Achievement Medals, Combat Action Ribbon, Good Conduct Medal, Humanitarian Service Medal, National Defense Service Medal, Afghanistan Campaign Medal, NATO Medal and the Global War on Terror Service Medal.

It is evident that Ramona Fowler birthed a baby boy and raised a Hero. The love, the respect, the sentiments said and unspoken, the fellow soldiers who pressed their way through the sea of other fellow Marines and Navy soldiers with tears in their eyes and heaviness in their hearts, just to say, "I'm sorry for your loss, I knew Brian, I was with Brian in Afghanistan, I'll always remember Brian, I loved Brian, …", was almost too much for any heart to bear. Ramona raised a Hero; that is evident. "That Boy", as she so lovingly referred to her son, is a Hero. He lived life, he loved life, he touched the hearts of so, so many, he encouraged others, he caused laughter, he was an example, he was generous, he was a helper, he inspired hope, "That Boy", as Mona called him is a Hero. As we quietly returned home, I reflected on just what it takes to raise a Hero! Surely, while giving birth has a significant place, is it enough to make a Hero; Perhaps the unconditional love of family, great nurturing, protection, teaching, training, communicating, or maybe a lot of discipline and much praying. I am persuaded that whatever it entails, raising a Hero has to be an awesome and all consuming task and yet, we know that it is possible; Mona raised a son but Brian died a Hero, because the Lord pre-destined him to be nothing less.

"For Your Information"

On Monday, April 2, 2012, our very own **Valerie Climons Caldwell**, **Esq**., was sworn into the Supreme Court Bar Association. Valerie is the wife of our very own John T. Caldwell, son of the late Hudson and Anner Lou Caldwell. Together, Val and John cherish the love of one daughter, Dr. Gabriella Caldwell Miller, son-in-law, Rev. Aamon Miller, one son, Jamal Caldwell and three beautiful grand-daughters. Valerie is a hard-working, dedicated wife, mother, grandmother, legal servant in her community and spiritual servant in her local church. She is also an awesome songstress, as demonstrated in her CD production entitled, "You Are So Beautiful". Valerie is a mentor, an inspiration, a fierce scrabble player and more importantly, she is a friend.

Congratulations Valerie Climons Caldwell, Esq.

Creighton Wallace

MrWallace.Bandcamp.com

Released 09 April 2011   Recorded, mixed and mastered by Double Impact Productions, January 2011. All songs written by Renske de Boer/Rudmer Gietema and Mr. Wallace. Produced by Mr. Wallace and Double Impact Productions. Cover design by Glashouwerdesign. Picture by Inge Nicolaij. http://www.mrwallace.nl/nl/home.html

Creighton is the son of Tommy Wallace, Sr. of Heflin, Louisiana. He works and resides in Fort Worth, TX. Creighton is on facebook, stop by, introduce yourself and say hello to Creighton!

Congratulations Mr. Wallace

Faith & Endurance

Shared by Jasmine R. Rice

Behold, we count them happy which endure. Ye have heard of the patience of Job, and have seen the end of the Lord; that the Lord is very pitiful, and of tender mercy. - James 5:11

The end, or purpose, of the Lord for his people is full of pity and tenderness. When we feel deeply afflicted, it is hard for us to believe that God is tenderly involved in our lives. We feel as though perhaps God has forsaken us or -- worse stil -- is punishing us for some mistake we have made. Job, as he was enduring the pain and sorrow of his lengthy ordeal, felt as if he had been utterly forsaken by God. Yet by faith he trusted in God, saying, "He knoweth the way that I take: when he hath tried me, I shall come forth as gold" (23:10). He relied on God's good purposes, in the midst of personal pain and loss and anguish. This is a difficult exercise, because it means living entirely by faith, regardless of our present circumstances. It means trusting God and patiently waiting for him to fulfill his perfect and merciful purposes for us. It means tenaciously holding to a heavenly and eternal perspective, rather than seeking pleasure and fulfillment here and now.

But the example of Job should remind us that even when grief or turmoil, hide the face of God from us, he is still working tenderly toward our sanctification and glory.

For this reason, James declares, we count them happy which endure. Those who steadfastly endure the trials God sends their way are, in the end, the most blessed people on earth. Their lives have brought glory to God, their testimony has pointed to eternity, and their faithfulness has reminded us of God's goodness.

ABOUT WINN PARISH, LOUISIANA

Winn Parish, Louisiana was created by legislative act in 1852, carved from portions of Natchitoches, Catahoula, and Rapides Parishes, therefore, the first census of Winn Parish was taken in 1860. Sadly, Schedule 2, Slave Inhabitants, enumerated in June and July, 1860, and taken by Rowell D. Wall, Assistant Marshal, lists no slave names. The name of the slave owner, the number of slaves owned, the age, sex, color ("B" for black, "M" for mixed or mulatto),whether or not the slave was a "fugitive from the state", whether or not the slave was manumitted (freed), whether or not the slave had an infirmity (deaf, dumb, blind, insane, or idiotic) and the number of slave houses are listed on the schedule. Sadly, the names of the slaves are not listed.

It is impossible to tell the address, or area, of the residence of the slave owner, unless one is familiar with early Winn Parish homesteads, which could possibly be occupied today, or in recent years, by the slave owner's descendants. Interestingly, there are many households with only one slave and hardly any at all with large numbers of slaves. Only two families owned more than 100 slaves and two more families owned more than sixty. This adds credence to the long held belief that Winn Parish was relatively poor in its infancy. Many will argue that to be the case today.

Webster Parish is a parish located in the northwestern section of the U.S. state of Louisiana. As of the 2010 census, the population was 41,207.[1] The seat of the parish is Minden.[2]

The parish is named for 19th-century American statesman Daniel Webster of Massachusetts and New Hampshire. It was created on February 27, 1871[3] from lands formerly belonging to Bienville, Bossier, and Claiborne parishes. Webster Parish is part of the Shreveport-Bossier City, LA Metropolitan Statistical Area. Among the first settlers in Webster Parish was Newett Drew, a native of Virginia, who about 1818 established a grist mill at the former Overton community near Minden. At this time the area was Natchitoches Parish and later Overton became the Parish Seat of Claiborne Parish in 1836 until it moved in 1848. His son, Richard Maxwell Drew was born in Overton and served as a district judge state representative prior to his death in 1850 at the age of twenty-eight. R. M. Drew's descendants held judicial or legislative positions in Webster Parish as well, Richard Cleveland Drew, Harmon Caldwell Drew, R. Harmon Drew, Sr., and Harmon Drew, Jr.[4]

My Brother's Keeper!

"Am I my brother's keeper?" Asked Cain, when questioned by God. It was a rhetorical question, Cain knew the answer or what he thought was the answer, it was "no" as far as he was concerned. Abel was dead, no need for keeping any more

"Am I my brother's keeper?" We ask, as we walk by the homeless man, standing in a doorway with his dog,
drinking our $4 latte. It's a rhetorical question; we think we know the answer. It's "no" as far as we're concerned
it's probably his fault he's homeless, why does he have a dog anyway? Why doesn't he get a job or at least go to a shelter for help instead of begging

"Am I my brother's keeper?" We ask, as we switch the channel, so we don't have to see the ad about children in Africa dying of diseases that are unheard of in our cozy little town. It's a rhetorical question, we think we know the answer it's "no" as far as we're concerned. Organizations like World Vision will take care of the dying children It's not our concern, we have Reality TV to watch, so we flip the channel again

"Am I my brother's keeper?" We ask, as the collection plate passes by. As we sit in our pew at the back of the church. It's a rhetorical question, we think we know the answer it's "no" as far as we're concerned. We drop in a $1 bill, that'll do. The other folks in the congregation can take up the slack. We need a new computer, a new car, maybe a new watch and the mortgage payment on our 5 bedroom house is coming due.

"Am I my brother's keeper?" We ask, as we skim our Facebook on our brand new computer and see a wall post about sex trafficking of young girls. It's a rhetorical question; we think we know the answer. It's "no" as far as we're concerned we don't engage in such activities and there's nothing we can do to stop it. It happens half way around the world and we're much too busy with our own lives Oh look, a new Facebook game to play

"Am I my brother's keeper?" It's not a rhetorical question; it's a real question, an important question. It's a question Jesus has answered and the answer is "YES".
"....... Inasmuch as ye have done it unto one of the least of these my brethren, ye have done it unto me".

We are our Brothers' keeper & our Sisters' keeper
Because we
"ARE"
Our Brothers and Sisters

"Makers of Men"

Jurlean Fowler Avery

At dawns early light, as I listened real close, I'd hear his big, strong, but gentle footsteps making their way throughout;
stopping to peak in this room, the next and then the next. He would pause a bit, here and there, as if taking note of some matter of importance, then he would resume his steps. Out a door, he would exit. In summer, it was hard to follow his steps, for the earth was soft and pliable, but in the Fall it seemed as if I could trace his footsteps all the way to heaven, that was his destination, for the crisp sounds of leaves would mark his every glide. While his stride seemed as long as he was tall, his pace was slow, but sure. Even outside, he would stop, walk, slow, and resume his pace again. I wondered, what did he see, that caused him to hesitate or stop, what caught his eye, what captured his attention. When he had gone full circle around the house, he would often journey a few paces up or down the street and join another of his species, who had, I assumed, likewise taken a similar journey around their own abode. They would share a morning handshake, looked all about as they talked a bit, and each turning back in the direction of his origin, return to their still, sleeping family. Well, almost, everyone was still sleeping. One year, one faithful day, when I heard him rustling and readying himself for this early morning ritual, I hastily dressed myself, determined to accompany him on this day break excursion. I don't know if he knew that from birth, I observed him, almost as much as he observed me. I liked the way he did things, said things, smiled, laughed, joked, and even when he chastised. I found him interesting, encouraging, likeable, and loveable. I wanted to be with him, around him, and know stuff that he knew. I needed to know why he awoke early mornings, what that journey around and outside of the house was about, what made him pause, what did he see, and if he did anything about whatever he saw. I just needed to know! Though I was only 5 or 6 at the time, the day that I decided to accompany him became a transformation in our relationship. I thought that he would scold me for getting up and perhaps send me back to bed, but somehow, I just knew that once he was sufficiently satisfied with my reason, he would say, in his own words "Well o.k., come along, if that's what you want", and so I did. I went along. Now seeing, what I had only previously heard and imagined, he said that he peeked in all the rooms to make sure that everyone was still

"accounted for", as they had been the night before; to see the "condition" of each room; messy, clean, organized, or whatever. (This was a former military man that ran a tight ship!). I did not quite understand all of his interest in such things, but I trusted him, and after all, this was my first time accompanying him on what seemed to be a pretty important mission, so for me, I was merely observing him, observing. Once we were outside, I learned that he would walk with both hand clasped behind him. I didn't quite understand that, but he did it, so I did it. When he paused, I paused. Each time he looked up, my head went up, when he stopped, I stopped. At some point, I decided that I would hold all of my questions for another time, for now, I was just content watching and being with him. He was fairly open for conversation, and especially on what I always considered Friday Night Family Night. Being the youngest of four kids, as the others grew old enough to go out at night, it seemed like it would be forever before I would be old enough to go anywhere, so Friday Night Family Night was as much fun as I could look forward to. Sometimes we would play Dominoes; that was his favorite game; other times, a card game called "Tunk", or watch TV, especially if Black people were going to be on, as that was rare in those days. Then other times we would just talk and boy could he talk; about everything, about anything, he just knew stuff! So, I would save my million questions until then, and from my many questions and over our lifetime of talks, I learned that my father, this man that I looked up to, and still adore even now, that he took a morning stroll around the house, inside and out, because he was the Man of the house, and that's the kind of thing that a Man does; A Man inspects his home to assure that everyone and everything is right where they/it should be, that no hurt, harm or danger had befell anyone or anything over the course of the night. I learned that the ritual of grasping his hands behind his back as he walked, was merely a habit he inherited, he said it relaxed him as he walked, so he didn't fight it, but one day I noticed, that he no longer held his hands behind his back, but as we walked, he held my hand, because as a man, and as my dad, he wanted me to feel safe and comforting. I learned that he would pause at times, to simply look at the wonders of God; a striking sunrise, the maturing of the Fall foliage, or the glistening of a new fallen snow. Other times, he stopped because he saw something perhaps out of order, or requiring further inspection. I learned that often as he walked, he talked to God, about all sorts of things; work, mom, him-self, the world, and even about me. I learned that he liked being a man and he loved being a husband and a father. I learned that he liked learning and he liked teaching. I learned that just because I was a girl, I could still do lots of stuff. I learned that it was just fine to have hopes and dreams. I learned that there had been times in his life when he had been hurt, both physically and emotionally, but more important than his hurts, he knew forgiveness. I learned that I could always trust and depend on him; he showed me that I could. I learned that when he was not there to talk to me or answer all of my questions that I could talk to God, and he would hear me; I learned that because he was a man, he had faults, shortcomings and failures, but he knew how to get back up. I learned that I was blessed, because my father, a man, was a blessing.

I don't know what all it takes to "Make A Man", though I'm sure that God and my grandpa had a lot to do with it, but what I know for sure, is that they made, one heck of a fine Man when they made my Dad.

In Remembrance of my Dad, Theodore Henderson Fowler
February 15, 1914 – September 12, 1997
May You Rest In Heavenly Peace

My Personal Views on Our Country's Problems
by John T. Caldwell

This article marks the first time that I have publicly expressed my personal moral and political views in any type of written media. There are so many issues that are affecting us nowadays that I was moved to let those people closest to me, my family, know what is on my mind. The issues that I would like to reflect on are the economy, immigration, gays in the military, and education. Although several chapters could be written on any one of these issues, I will, at best, present my viable summary.

Starting with the economy, the term that you hear the most is "creating more jobs". Although this term does have validity, it cannot be a literal solution. Before we begin creating those jobs, we need to either create new businesses or promote business expansions. When I think of "creating jobs" as a standalone objective, I think of my Army basic training experience of moving large rocks from one side of the road to the opposite side. On the next day, our platoon sergeant would have us move those large rocks back to the other side of the road. To me this was a classic example of creating work; however, years later, after I had left the service I realized that this was a military method for instilling discipline. Although this made sense for the military, it has no place in a sagging economy without the presence of a real increase in business activity.

At a time when business activity needs to increase to boost our economy, we find that existing businesses are downsizing and outsourcing overseas, while the banks are very reluctant to finance any new business, especially entrepreneurs. So, you ask yourself, if the existing businesses are getting smaller or shifting their labor forces to another country and the banks are indifferent to new businesses, then where can the new jobs possibly appear?

My proposed solution in this case is twofold: first, the existing businesses need to be more positive and creative by looking to increase sales, rather than reducing expenses by downsizing. As the old adage goes, nobody makes money until somebody sells something. Therefore, companies should innovate by enlisting all of their employees, regardless of department, into being part of the company's sales force. Should this happen; all the employees in the company will be empowered to help increase the growth of the company and control their own destiny. The other part of the solution is that the banks should be given some type of tax incentive or government underwriting guarantee to support new and emerging businesses that prove themselves worthy. I feel that this, if successful, will have a direct effect of increasing jobs.

Concerning immigration, I feel that the predominate attitude in this country is negative and exclusive. Although immigration can be legal or illegal, it appears that the word "immigration" has become synonymous with "illegal immigrant". Our overall response to the illegal immigrants is to ascertain that they get no jobs, no health care, no government benefits, and no education.
With so many "no's", many of these immigrants become our financial dependents in our prison industry, costing us millions.
Also, since we have no efficient means to export them back to their home country, wouldn't it make sense to give them the best path possible to become productive and pay into our "soon to be broke" social security system? Imagine the ingenuity it must have taken to cross the border   to come into this country and then imagine how creative these same people could be if they were allowed to participate in our controlled labor force, where they will pay taxes, and allowed to create businesses, which will also be taxed. With a large portion of American workers, the "baby boomers", going into retirement (collecting Social Security payments), with a much smaller pool of younger workers paying into the Social Security fund, we need more highly productive younger people, to include immigrants, to replenish the Social Security reserves. So, in essence, instead of fearing that immigrants take American jobs, I prefer to look at them as business and job creators, if we could only remove our negative defenses and figure out ways to get them as productive as possible in a short period of time.

Concerning gays in the military, for me that is a "no brainer". We often hear the argument about not allowing an openly gay person the "honor" of servicing in the military. However, for anybody who has ever served in a military war zone, you do not think about the "honor" until you are taking your bows outside of that war zone in front of an admiring audience. But, while you were busy ducking enemy fire, you do not care whether your comrade, who is helping you return enemy fire, is a man, a woman, or a homosexual. In addition, if the fighting gets too heated, you would like to know that your comrade-in- arms would not be able to leave you fighting on the battlefield by saying, "I'm gay,

I want out". Therefore, I think the right to honor and the right to shed blood on the battlefield should be equal, whether man, woman, or gay.

Finally, looking at education, I think that this is the key to America's future as well as the long term key to curing the problems with our economy. Not only do I think that we should spend more money on education, but we should make education available to everybody in this country who wants an education, to include immigrants. When you look at where the U.S. stands among other industrialized nations, to include China and Japan, our educational system and our technology are lagging more and more. Speaking briefly about technology, China now has the fastest train in the world, at over 300 miles per hour, while our fastest train, the Amtrak Acela Express can only travel up to 150 miles per hour. As China, Japan, and India are spending more money on education, the U.S. is consistently spending less. So, if we stay on the same path, by the next generation we will be the most advanced new "Third World" country on the planet. It is about time that we start spending more money on schools and education than we are spending on building and maintaining prisons.

Of all of the issues that I addressed, I think that education and how it is administered, has to be the most important key to turning our country and our economy around.

Men

What they see is what they do

All that is necessary for the triumph of evil is that good men do nothing.
Edmund Burke

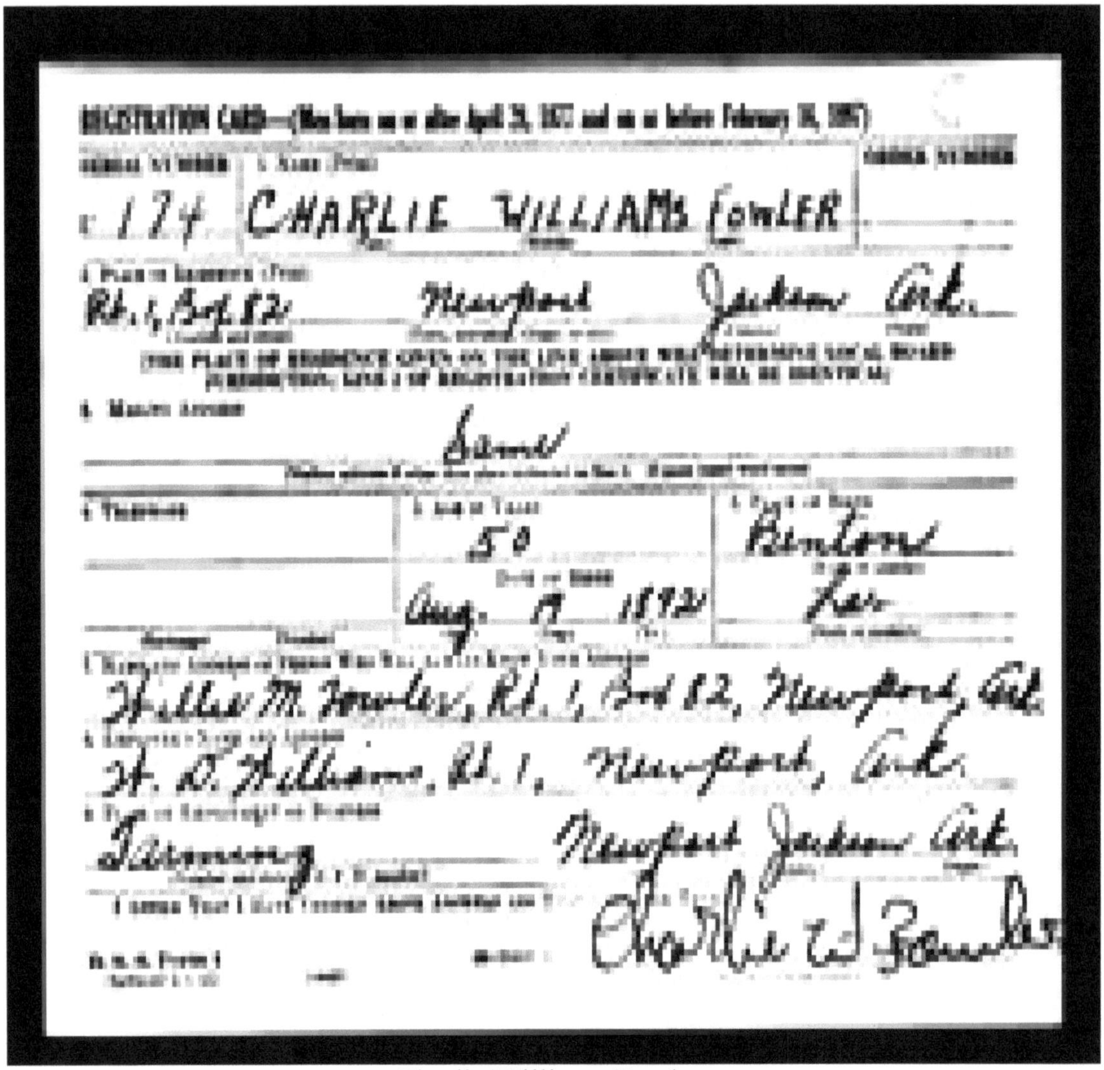

REGISTRATION CARD

174 CHARLIE WILLIAMS FOWLER

Rt. 1, Box 82 Newport Jackson Ark.

Same

50

Benton

Aug. 19 1892

Willie M. Fowler, Rt. 1, Box 82, Newport, Ark.

H. D. Williams, Rt. 1, Newport, Ark.

Farming Newport Jackson Ark.

Charlie W Fowler

Charlie Williams Fowler

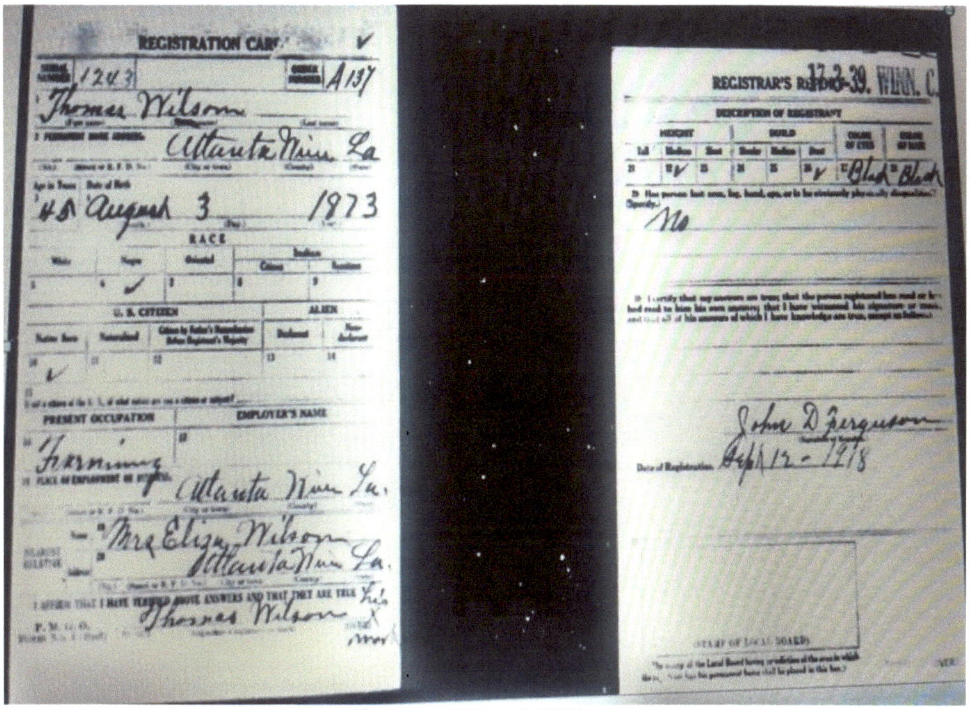
REGISTRATION CARD
1243
A137
Thomas Wilson
Atlanta Winn La
45 August 3 1873
RACE
U. S. CITIZEN
ALIEN
PRESENT OCCUPATION
EMPLOYER'S NAME
Farming
Atlanta Winn La.
Mrs Eliza Wilson
Atlanta Winn La.
I AFFIRM THAT I HAVE VERIFIED ABOVE ANSWERS AND THAT THEY ARE TRUE
Thomas Wilson
his X mark
P. M. G. O.
REGISTRAR'S REPORT 17-3-39. WINN
DESCRIPTION OF REGISTRANT
HEIGHT
BUILD
Black
Black
No
John D Ferguson
Date of Registration Sept 12 - 1918
STAMP OF LOCAL BOARD

Thomas (Tom) Wilson

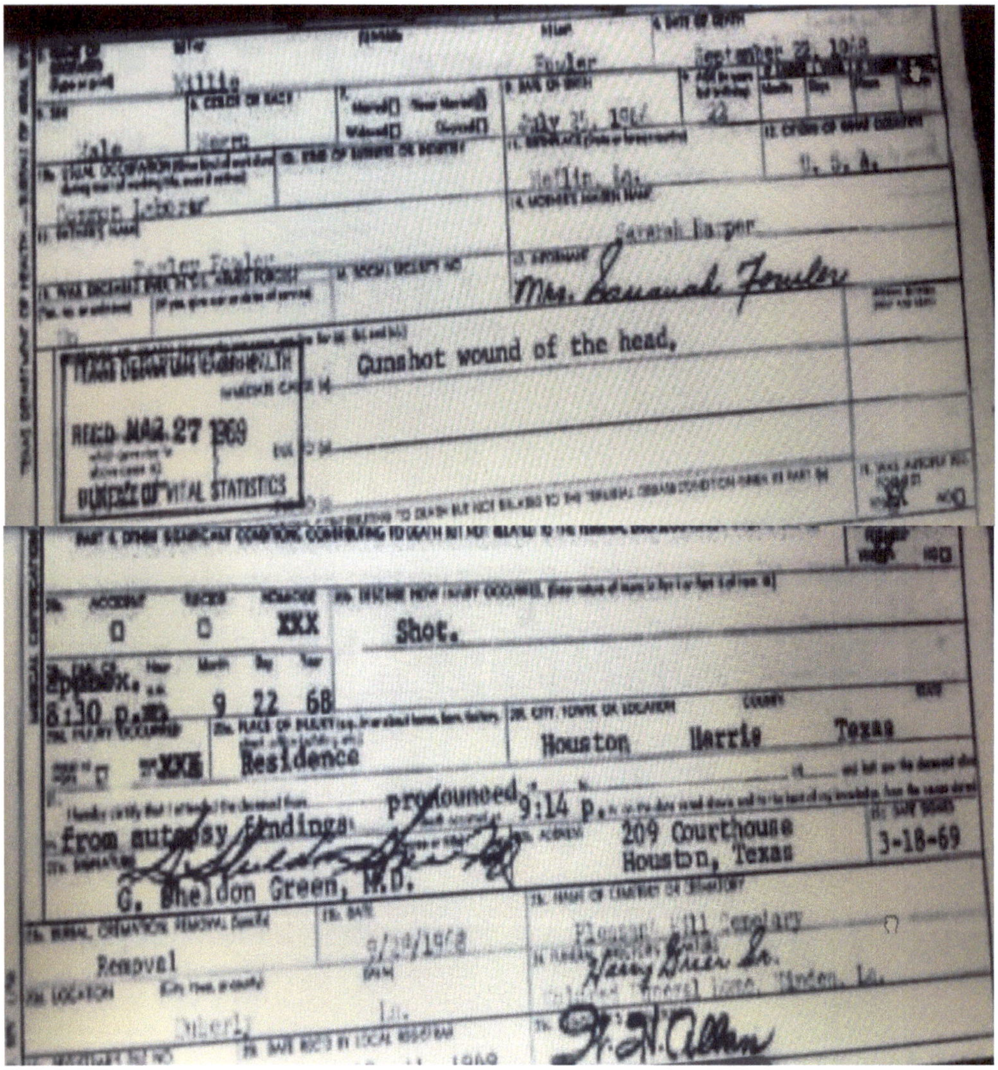

Willie Fowler

Form 1 *1693* REGISTRATION CARD No. *59*

1 Name in full *Cleveland Fowler* Age in yrs. *23*
   (Given name) (Family name)

2 Home address *Dubberly* *La*
   (No.) (Street) (City) (State)

3 Date of birth *about Dec about 20* *1894*
   (Month) (Day) (Year)

4 Are you (1) a natural-born citizen, (2) a naturalized citizen, (3) an alien, (4) or have you declared your intention (specify which)? *Natural Born*

5 Where were you born? *Dubberly La USa*
   (Town) (State) (Nation)

6 If not a citizen, of what country are you a citizen or subject?

7 What is your present trade, occupation, or office? *Log Cawyer 18*

8 By whom employed? *Wossard & Walker*
   Where employed? *Dubberly*

9 Have you a father, mother, wife, child under 12, or a sister or brother under 12, solely dependent on you for support (specify which)? *None*

10 Married or single (which)? *Single* Race (specify which)? *Colored*

11 What military service have you had? Rank *None*; branch ; years ; Nation or State

12 Do you claim exemption from draft (specify grounds)? *None*

I affirm that I have verified above answers and that they are true.

Cleveland Fowler
(Signature or mark)

1395 17-3-37. Webster, A.
REGISTRAR'S REPORT

1 Tall, medium, or short (specify which)? *Med* Slender, medium, or stout (which)? *Med*

2 Color of eyes? *Blk* Color of hair? *Blk* Bald? *No*

3 Has person lost arm, leg, hand, foot, or both eyes, or is he otherwise disabled (specify)? *No*

I certify that my answers are true, that the person registered has read his own answers, that I have witnessed his signature, and that all of his answers of which I have knowledge are true, except as follows:

C.a Batton
(Signature of registrar)

Precinct *7*
City or County *Webster*
State *La*

6/5/17
(Date of registration)

Cleveland Fowler

Sgt. Maj. Mark Byrd

Date: 10.18.2009   **Posted:** 11.03.2009 11:23   **News ID:** 41012

KANDAHAR AIRFIELD, Kandahar province, Afghanistan — Deployed service members are able to communicate better than ever with their loved ones, through internet, phone centers and satellite phones, but for one Marine all it took was a quick flight.

Sgt. Maj. Mark Byrd Sr., sergeant major of Marine Light Attack Helicopter Squadron 169, Marine Aircraft Group 40, Marine Expeditionary Brigade-Afghanistan, was reunited with his son, Senior Airman Mark Byrd Jr., an airframes mechanic, 451st Expeditionary Aeromedical Evacuation Flight, 451st Air Expeditionary Wing, here Oct. 18.

The unique visit allowed the two, who are commonly confused as brothers, to talk football and reflect on their time in the military.

"I see him more here than I do at home," joked Mark Sr., who is currently stationed at Camp Leatherneck, Helmand province.

The military upbringing Mark Jr. experienced provided him experiences his father never had.

"For my first 18, 19 years all I knew was Pontiac, Mich.," said Mark Sr., referring to the less diverse area. "My kids grew up with all people and all cultures. [The military lifestyle] developed me and it developed my family."

Hard work was a staple in the Byrd household, and Mark Sr. ensured his home always had a garage gym for his children and the neighborhood kids.

"If you come you are going to work. I don't play in the gym," said Mark Sr., who not only competed in high school wrestling and football, but coached as well.

Reflecting on the past, both father and son agreed on the best duty station of Mark Sr.'s career.

"My most rewarding time in the Marine Corps was on the drill field. Seeing the transformation of recruits is very rewarding," said Mark Sr.

Mark Sr. set an example for his son, in between training recruits all hours of the day, Mark Sr. was an assistant coach on Mark Jr.'s high school football and wrestling teams.

"I take everything from my dad. One thing I knew in particular growing up, is that my father was never a hypocrite," said Mark Jr., 25.

Now, Mark Jr. is developing his own career as an airframe mechanic on unmanned aerial vehicles, fighter jets, transport aircraft and helicopters.

Looking toward the future, Mark Sr. doesn't see his family's service to its country dwindling.

"I see myself as the beginning of something big," said Mark Sr. "We've had other older relatives in the Army and Marine Corps, but I think what we've got going in our family is the epitome of being an American," said Mark Sr.

Although Mark Jr. didn't choose the same branch of service as his father, Mark Sr. has high hopes that his son, Quamaine, a college student in Pennsylvania will become one of the few and the proud.

"If Quamaine joined, it would be the Marine Corps," said Mark Sr.

Although Mark Sr. has great pride in being a Marine, no hostility is shown toward Mark Jr. for joining another service.

"It is an honorable thing is to serve the country, regardless of branch of service," said Mark Sr.

Mark Jr. initially wanted to join the Marine Corps, but after Mark Sr. advised him to visit all the recruiters, Mark Jr. settled on the Air Force.

The bonus and accelerated promotion enticed Mark Jr., who said the Air Force is a "totally different lifestyle," than the Marine Corps.

After living the military life growing up, Mark Jr. has now seen his own fair share of places while serving in the Air Force. Besides Afghanistan, Mark Jr. has been to Texas, Florida, Oklahoma, Nevada and Korea in his seven years of service.

U.S. World War II Army Enlistment Records, 1938-1946

Theodore Henderson Fowler

Name:	Theo H Fowler
Birth Year:	1914
Race:	Negro, citizen (Black)
Nativity State or Country:	Louisiana
State of Residence:	Louisiana
County or City:	Webster
Enlistment Date:	25 Apr 1942
Enlistment State:	Louisiana
Enlistment City:	Camp Livingston
Branch:	Branch Immaterial - Warrant Officers, USA
Branch Code:	Branch Immaterial - Warrant Officers, USA
Grade:	Private
Grade Code:	Private
Term of Enlistment:	Enlistment for the duration of the War or other emergency, plus six months, subject to the discretion of the President or otherwise according to law
Component:	Selectees (Enlisted Men)
Source:	Civil Life
Education:	3 years of high school
Marital Status:	Single, without dependents
Height:	67
Weight:	142

U.S., World War I Draft Registration Cards, 19

17-1918 Napoleon Phillips

Name:	Napoleon Phillips
County:	Winn
State:	Louisiana
Birthplace:	Louisiana, United States of America
Birth Date:	
Race:	Black

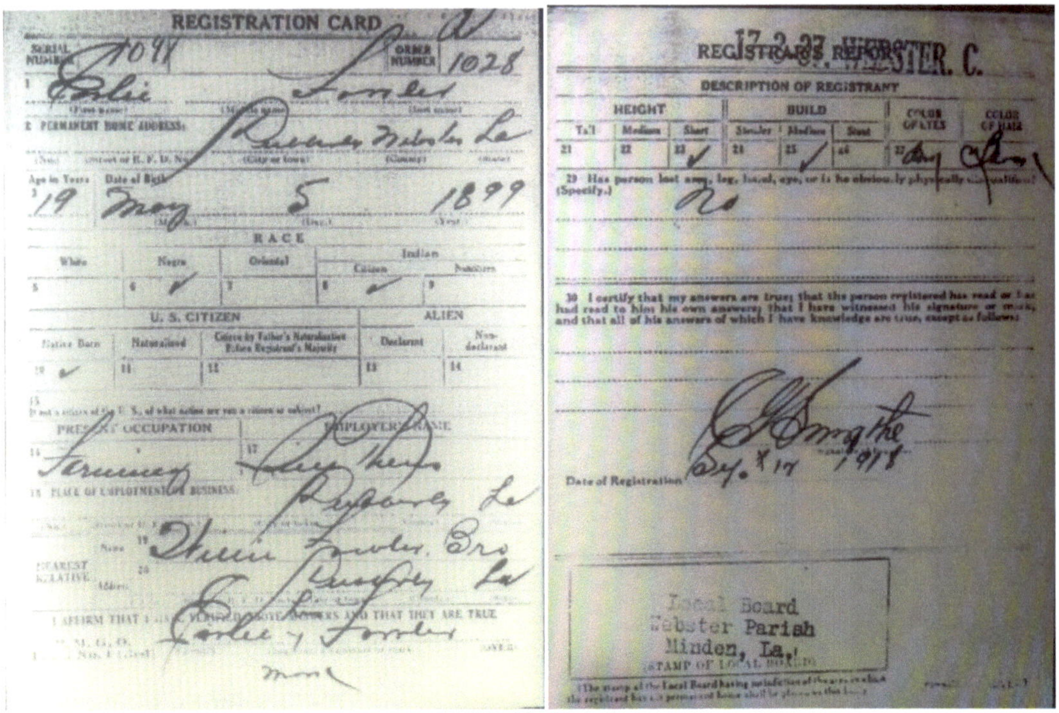

REGISTRATION CARD

SERIAL NUMBER 1044 ORDER NUMBER 1028

1 Earlie Fowler
(First name) (Middle name) (Last name)

2 PERMANENT HOME ADDRESS: Webster La

Age in Years 19 Date of Birth May 5 1899

RACE

White	Negro	Oriental	Indian Citizen	Indian Noncitizen
5	6 ✓	7	8 ✓	9

U. S. CITIZEN			ALIEN	
Native Born	Naturalized	Citizen by Father's Naturalization Before Registrant's Majority	Declarant	Non-declarant
10 ✓	11	12	13	14

15 If not a citizen of the U. S., of what nation are you a citizen or subject?

PRESENT OCCUPATION: 16 Farming

EMPLOYER'S NAME: 17

18 PLACE OF EMPLOYMENT OR BUSINESS: La

NEAREST RELATIVE: Name 19 Fowler, Bro. Address 20 La

I AFFIRM THAT I HAVE VERIFIED ABOVE ANSWERS AND THAT THEY ARE TRUE

Earlie Fowler

REGISTRAR'S REPORT 17-2-37 WEBSTER C.

DESCRIPTION OF REGISTRANT

HEIGHT			BUILD			COLOR OF EYES	COLOR OF HAIR
Tall	Medium	Short	Slender	Medium	Stout		
21	22	23 ✓	24	25 ✓	26	27	

29 Has person lost arm, leg, hand, eye, or is he obviously physically disqualified? (Specify.) No

30 I certify that my answers are true; that the person registered has read or has had read to him his own answers; that I have witnessed his signature or mark, and that all of his answers of which I have knowledge are true, except as follows:

Smythe

Date of Registration Sept 12 1918

Local Board
Webster Parish
Minden, La.
(STAMP OF LOCAL BOARD)

Earlie Fowler

From the Research of
Mr. Stafford Davis

Descendant William "Bill" (Jess) Phillips, Sr. William "Bill" (Jess) Phillip was born in Charleston, South Carolina to Ms. Eliza (Jess) Phillips.

He remembered their last name being "Jess" during slavery. Shortly after the abolishment of slavery, Bill and his mother joined a group of people named Phillips that were moving from South Carolina to Louisiana. During this period they changed their names from Jess to Phillips. Bill's sisters Laura Goff and Edith moved to Emden, Louisiana with him and his mother.

There his mother married Mr. Jack Sapp; six children were born to this union, Louis, Kitty, Ben, Eli, Rose Ann, and Elvy. In 1874 Bill married Ms. Francis (Brown) Peats in Winn Parish, Louisiana. To this union nine children were born: twins, General Lee "Dad" and Eliza "Liza", Isabella "Isa", Arlevia "Levia", Emanuel "Sam", William "Bill" Jr., Napoleon Alexander "Coot", Raymond, and Lisbon "Shorty".

Bill was a blacksmith, carpenter, farmer, and deacon as well as a dentist. Several blacksmith items and a pair of tooth pulling pliers he made are still in the family.

The state accredited one-room Phillips School, Bethlehem Baptist Church and cemetery near Atlanta, Winn Parish, Louisiana, were constructed with Bill's leadership and land donation.

On February 10, 2000 this school was placed on the National Register of Historic Places. The records of this school can be found in the Winn Parish Board Office, Winnfield, Louisiana. The dedication and unveiling of the historic marker at this site was held Saturday, May 6, 2000.

Winn Parish Enterprise/News-American

"Winn-Then" by, Greggory E. Davies, Winnfield, LA.)
Preston Powell was born on Friday, October 23, 1936 in Winnfield , LA

Pinecrest High School, Winnfield's school for black students prior to its closing in 1969 due to integration, produced some of the greatest athletes and athletic teams Louisiana has ever known. One of the great athletes, Preston Powell is still a huge, physically fit man. His brothers, the late Haston and the late Narvin, were both great athletes as well. The third brother, Bobby, blind since childhood and unable to compete athletically, is a long time national recording artist. Another generation of the Powell's passed through the Winnfield Senior High School system and like their fathers, were great athletes.

Preston Powell is now 58 years old and lives in Cleveland, Ohio. he graduated from Pinecrest in 1957 and was the "Yellow jacket" quarterback. His senior year, Pinecrest lost to Zachary in the state finals. His junior year, they lost to Haynesville in the state semi-finals. Another great athlete from Pinecrest, or Winn Training School as Pinecrest was initially named, was Fred Hobdy who had a good career at Grambling, later becoming the basketball coach, still later the athletic director. Hobdy saw talent in Preston Powell and signed him to play basketball for Grambling. A feud erupted when Powell arrived at Grambling as the football coach, the legendary Eddie Robinson, basketball coach Hobdy, and baseball coach and college president Ralph Waldo Emerson Jones, Jr., argued over which sport Powell would play for the school. Naturally, President Jones won the argument and Powell played baseball, but was allowed to play football as well. Powell states today that his greatest regret is that he fell twenty-one hours short of graduation. Powell played quarterback for two years at Grambling before moving to running back where he earned All-America honors two years in a row. Drafted by the Cleveland Browns in the 6th round, he played there under the legendary Paul Brown for two years. The Browns traded Powell to the Dallas Cowboys where played a season under Tom Landry before being traded to Chicago where he played under still another legend, George Halas. The Browns won the world championship the year Powell left and the Bears won while he was on that squad, but he was injured and had to watch the game from the sidelines.

Football was not the only sport Powell excelled in. He is enshrined in the National Softball Hall of Fame in Ohio, and the St. Louis Cardinal baseball organization tried to steal him from Grambling, but President Jones refused to allow him to sign a contract. Following a football career ending injury, Powell was given the opportunity to play minor league baseball but refused as he thought it would have taken him too long to make the "big show". Powell said he loves coming home to what he calls "a fine place, Winnfield, where I have a lot of good friends." Eleven games short of an NFL pension, Powell has worked in public service since leaving the game. He has spent eleven years with the Cuyahoga County, Ohio Sheriff's Office, two years with the Ohio State Parole Department, and the past fifteen years with the City of Cleveland Rehabilitation & Probation. Powell said football had opened up so many opportunities for him and that he had been fortunate enough to have met and played for many legends. He added that Jim Brown was the greatest player he has ever known, having missed only five minutes of nine seasons, and only then Powell said "because he was knocked out cold." He went on to say that today's athletes were faster, stronger, more physical, and that is the reason for so many injuries. "I was given $ 3,500 as a signing bonus, and the most I ever made in a year was $40,000. A career can end in a split second so I strongly emphasize to young people to stay in school, get educated, and do something with their lives."

VOICE

Written by Janice Byrd-Rice for Women Everywhere

Before you entered this grand stage called LIFE you had VOICE. It was a gift from God. It cried out as you made your entrance and screamed loudly, "I am here!" But this voice, your voice; it is capable of speaking without sound. This voice is the quiet confidence that SHINES forth in your countenance. It is the elegance in your gait as you stroll into a room. It is the power of persuasion you exude in your speech.

It threatens many among you; your silent and not so silent adversaries all seeking what you have – VOICE. The enemy tried to silence it with every hurt, with every disappointment, and with every plot directed toward you. The enemy tried to give your voice over to jealousy, envy and strife directed toward your fellow sisters. Oh he tried to give your voice hatred for every man for the mistakes of your father and every other man that did you wrong. He tried to mask it in anger, self-pity, and doubt. He tried to give it over to low self-esteem and self-image. But, God...He won't let my enemy defeat me! Your God...He won't let your enemy defeat you!

God gave me and you VOICE! It is not angry; it is not jealous; it is not hateful! It is the voice that whispers love and encouragement. It is a voice of strength. It is a voice of wisdom. It is a voice that cries out to protect her loved ones. It is the voice that inspires her children. And it is the voice that prays and reasons with our God on behalf of her family. It is the voice of faith, hope and patience.

So, my Sisters, take back your voice! Let go of the hurts and disappointments of the past, and look to your future with VOICE. Your future SHINES brighter than your past! Use your voice to speak life to your families, to uplift, to encourage and inspire them to be all that God desires of them. Do not give your VOICE to the enemy's plans. You are phenomenal and you are the Virtuous woman of God! You are valued above rubies and your VOICE is priceless!

Don't Forget to SHINE!

Written by Janice Byrd-Rice for Women Everywhere
2012 Fowler-Caldwell Family Reunion Women's Conference - Biloxi, MS, July 2012

StyleSeat

February 7, 2014

Kamilah Mabrey

Kamilah "Kay" Mabrey was born in Toledo, Ohio, where her passion for hair began. Raised by Jack and Sharon Mabrey, Kay was determined to follow the path of her Grandma as well as her Uncle Edwin "Sky" Mabrey. Kamilah enrolled herself into Herron's Beauty College in Toledo, Ohio, and soon obtained her Managing Cosmetology License in 2001. Working under her Uncle's wings for 17 years, she decided to venture out on her own and relocate to Georgia, in 2013 for other career opportunities.

The Commander of
Marine Corps Base Quantico
request the pleasure of your company at the
Sergeants Major Relief and Appointment
Ceremony
at which
Sergeant Major Laura L. Brown,
United States Marine Corps,
will relinquish her duties to
Sergeant Major Mark A. Byrd,
United States Marine Corps,
Wednesday,
the eighteenth of December
two thousand and thirteen
at two o'clock in the afternoon
at Little Hall Auditorium
Marine Corps Base
Quantico, Virginia
Welcome Reception
immediately following the ceremony at
The Clubs at Quantico

Breath of Life.......

by Marshalynn Byrd Johnson

To be created in an image of perfection by the "Potter"... Only the best ingredients will do; the perfect clay, the best water, mighty hands, and prophetic words. The hands of the creator work the potter's wheel with great anticipation... With every turn of the wheel he is pressing, shaping, framing, and curving every detail--- while speaking into existence with a mighty voice of power and authority his perfect will for his creation.

He has expectation, desire, and purpose for this creation...The wheel continues to turn--- he is molding, and marveling at the sight of the masterpiece forming before him. He continues to pour out of himself with his mighty and powerful voice the blessing over the masterpiece. Heaven and Earth which was created in the beginning are at "Awe" with the great work being done.

A masterpiece in the making......The final touches are applied to the magnificent masterpiece. As the potter's wheel comes to a halt, the creator pronounces the authority and power of the creation---"He shall have dominion over everything in the earth---he has the blessing, fruitfulness, multiplication, power and authority to replenish, and to subdue everything upon the earth.......

The creator breathed into the nostril of the masterpiece the breath of life......

Fowler-Caldwell-Wallace

While continuing my ancestral research, I was led to re-review all of the documents and information I previously located, and much to my surprise and delight, the very first document that records our ancestry, reveals the very likely clue of where we originated. According to the 1880 U.S. Census, Wilas Fowler (born about 1848) reported that his father was born in the Gullah Region of Georgia.

Located on the Sea Islands of Georgia and S. Carolina are communities of people known as Gullah and Geechie (Most refer to those in S. Carolina as Gullah, and those in Georgia as Geechie). Many years of research and findings have led historians to believe **that the slaves brought to those areas were taken from the Gola, a tribe from Sierra Leone, West Africa.** Remnants of these communities remain today, and they struggle to hold on to the language and cultures from their ancestral home land. The Gullah are known for preserving more of their African linguistic and cultural heritage than any other African-American community in the United States. They speak an English-based Creole language containing many African loanwords and significant influences from African languages in grammar and sentence structure. _This offers what I think is one feasible explanation for some of the many errors in the early U.S. Census records, particularly with regards to names and spelling of names. With their heavy accent, the names spoken by family members, was not easily comprehended by census takers, so they took great liberty in recording whatever they "thought" was being said. After the Civil War ended in 1865, slaves were freed. Since most plantation owners were not able to produce crops without slave labor, some of the land was sold to plantation workers. Most of those who remained on the islands made a living by farming and fishing. They had little contact with the mainland because the only way to travel off the island was by boat. Given this geographic isolation, Native Islanders were able to maintain their folkways and language.

Over the years, much of land was bought and modernized by wealthy Americans, and turned into areas we now know as resorts. Sadly, only about 1% of the land is still held, maintained and occupied by the descendants of slaves. Although many feel that their traditions and language are <u>endangered</u>, the Gullah have survived change and held onto their past. Fortunately, the Gullah/Geechee Cultural Preservation Act was signed into law in October 2006. It established a culture heritage corridor and created a commission to help federal, state, and local authorities manage it. Sponsored by the Native Island Business and Community Affairs Association, Inc. (NIBCAA), the Hilton Head Island Gullah Celebration is held on Hilton Head Island, SC. Additional Gullah festivals are celebrated with music, dance and storytelling traditions, in Beaufort, S.C. While researching our ancestry, it has been my continuous prayer that our ancestors speak to my heart and lead me on the right path from one family member to the next. I am utterly convinced, without a doubt that dear Wilas Fowler intended that we know our roots, spoke to my heart, and has indeed led us there.

Did You Celebrate When.......

By Jurlean Fowler Avery

Just recently, while relaxing and meditating on the goodness of our savior, I was quickened by the thought of all the many opportunities I had to celebrate, but for one reason or another, did not, acknowledged that positive in my life and moved on to the next chapter. That is really just another form of taking the goodness for granted and it is not the right thing to do. Certainly, I'm not suggesting that we halt the activities of daily living and throw a party every time something good happens in our life, but surely, we need to give it more than a nodding recognition. Life is short, tomorrow is not promised and there is sufficient heartbreak and sinister evil that consumes the bulk of our time and space every day, so when something good or anything positive happen, some degree of celebration or merriment should be in order.

Do you remember when you achieved your most recent goal; Did you celebrate! When you passed that test; Did you celebrate! When you planned, cooked and successfully presented your most recent Thanksgiving dinner, then stood observantly by while everyone enjoyed themselves; Did you celebrate! Perhaps you have been waiting for others to throw the celebration for you. Well, I don't want to be the one to disappoint you, but that's not likely to happen. Other people, even those closest to you can express their pride and joy for your success, but only "you" can really appreciate the toils and struggles you went through to achieve your goal and only "you" can truly know what it takes to make you feel good, uplifted and happy when you are triumphant. It's not vanity or arrogance, but rather, a simple course in gratitude. While it is normal and even important to expect that family and friends will ingratiate us when we pass a challenge, I think that we weigh too heavy on that expectation and of course, we are hurt and devastated when it does not happen.

When we learn to rejoice in our own up,s and just take a moment or so to baste in the glory of the goodness of God, no matter how large or small, I am fairly confident that our dependence upon others for feedback and acceptance will become less important and contain far less impact, when they do not occur.

So, the next time you achieve anything good, anything positive, exceed your next hurdle, climb your next mountain, overcome whatever, break through, conquer, defeat, crush, advance, win or simply move forward, take a space of time, acknowledge He who made you and do your happy dance!

"Twas The Life Before" ©

by Jurlean Fowler Avery

"It was" the life before freedom, for slaves, indentured servants, and
people of color everywhere.
Only a rumor of hope, a dream of liberty, and imagined independence
moved the air.
Though weary and worn, from their struggles and strain;
These were a people who believed, had hope, but knew great pain.
The pain of another day's labor, the ridicule, and whips; The degradation,
humiliation, and nightmare of slave ships.
The calls upon their God to save, send help, and not forsake them.
The waiting, wondering, and praying to Him.
How could this be; we have harmed no man, and committed no wrong,
their hearts would cry out.
Our women are raped, our children sold, and our home is no more; They
work us, beat us, and defile us, till we're sore.
Deliver us, we pray, from this existence we share.
Lead us far from here Please, do not forsake us, deliver us we pray, we
need you, repeatedly, they'd shout and let us know that you care.

At that exact moment, at the right time, and as destiny would have
known; Freedom came a calling, to lead a people home.
Perhaps not home to the land of their mothers, or familiar earth. But,
once set free, free at last, as if a new birth.
They would go well beyond the plantations they knew, some scattered
here and there.
Going north, east and west: but far away from their nightmare.

They dreamed and imagined, they surmised and assumed. They guessed
about tomorrow, their future, and all that loomed.
They saw newness of life, new love, grown from seeds of faith.
And though they shared loss, suffered great pain, the day of freedom was
not late.
It came when it came, the timing was right. Freedom was here; surely a
new day, a new light.
They danced, they shouted, and thanked their God above, for every little
thing, and especially his love.

We will work hard, they said, do well, be fruitful and multiply. Our children will tell the story, to assure that our legacy will never die.

They should always tell the story, of how we overcame;
To their children, their children's children, each and every one should know the same.
Tell them we had hope, strength, and our refusal to succumb. Make sure they know of our faith that this day would be won.
A day when our descendants; yes, you, your sisters and brothers, would be here to carry on, go forth, and teach one another.
Teach them to live their best moment, best day, and best life. Teach them to love, care for one another, have faith, and avoid strife.
Tell them that we love them; we have great hopes and dreams enough for you all,
Assure them that they can make it; they can succeed, achieve, and stand tall.
And even if some fall, you be there for them; encourage, pray, and let them drink from your cup.
Cheer them to get up again, like the warriors we are; and never, my love, don't ever, give up.

Twas the life before freedom, a life no one should ever know,
But we endured it all, we were strong, faithful, and we have proof to show.
It is You, my love, the result of all we endured;
And though we have passed on, just know and be sure, yes the story of your people, is true and it's pure.

So, stand up you Men, be phenomenal you Women, show them who you are, every boy and girl,
You have great work to do, marvels to behold, adventures await you, all over this world.
You are amazing, beautiful, gifted and strong; do not be discouraged, stay on the right path, and you will not go wrong.
You are endowed with history, greatness, and a wondrous story to tell,
For you, my love, are generations of The Family; Wilson, Phillips, Fowler, Wallace and Caldwell.

Louisiana, Marriages, 1718-1925

Tom Wilson & Eliza Phillips

Name:	Eliza Phillips
Spouse:	Tom Wilson
Marriage Date:	**6 Feb 1903**
Marriage Place:	Winn Parish

Katie Wilson & Holcomb Ford

Name:	Holcomb Ford
Spouse:	Katie Wilson
Marriage Date:	**22 Dec 1898**
Marriage Place:	Winn Parish

Irvin Wallace & Tamer Tillman

Name:	Irvin Wallace
Spouse:	Tamer Tillman
Marriage Date:	**2 Jan 1874**
Marriage Place:	Webster Parish

BEGOTTEN
Proudly Presenting
Faces of Hope

1909 PHOTO OF WILSON, PHILLIPS, SAPP'S & MORE IN ATLANTA, WINN PARISH, LOUISIANA

THE BETHLEHEM BAPTIST CHURCH (APX.-1909)

THE TILLMAN CHURCH FAMILY, HEFLIN, LOUISIANA

Duncan Wallace
1840 – Unknown

Antonio Lamar Ashford, Jr.
Late infant son of Antonio L. Ashford, Sr. and Charity Lemke
and brother of Lexis and Abregail Ashford
Birth 8 SEP 1993 in Chicago, Cook, Illinois
Death 29 JUNE 1995 in Chicago, Cook, Illinois

Attorney Carol Wilson Caldwell
26 Feb 1946 - 16 Apr 1976
Late wife of John Caldwell and mother of Dr. Gabriella Caldwell Miller
Pinelawn Cemetery
Bethel (Pitt County), Pitt County, North Carolina, USA

Ira Wilson & Marry Pearl Wilson

Henry Hall

Gabriella (Caldwell) & husband, Aamon Miller

Addie & son, Carlos Vercher

Ayriel & Alexys Bowie

Alton Wilson

Alicia & brother, Cedric Ivy

Andre' L. Fowler

Alyssa Coleman

Anner Lou Fowler Caldwell

Annie Ruth Fowler Lipkins

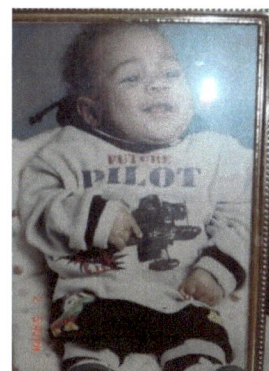

Antonio Lamar Ashford, Jr.

Antonio L. Ashford, Sr. & Tina Chatman-Ashford Antonio & Baby Abregail Ashford

Brothers, Ashton & Armond Hicks   & sister, Aubrey Talynn Hicks

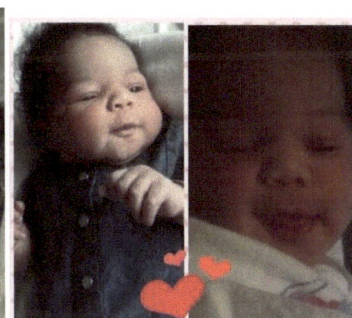

Austin Carter Pittman

Atkins Thomas Fowler

Betty Gene Fowler Brown

Betty Ruth Loud

Booker & wife, Billie Fowler

Brandee Bowie

Brandon and sister, Brittany Jackson

Brandon Caldwell

Brenda Ann Weathers Caldwell

Petty Officer 2nd Class Brian Keith Lundy Jr.
25 of Austin, Texas

Brian Keith Lundy, Jr.

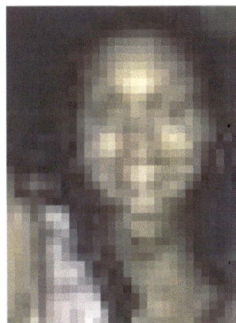

Brianne Garcia

Bridgett Fowler Garcia

Caelon and brother, Raelon Reed

Carolyn Jenae Miller

Camryn Miller

Carl J. Rice, Sr.

Carl J. Rice, Jr. (CJ)

Carlos Eugene Fowler Muhammad

Carmen Fowler

Carmonice Wallace

Carrie Wallace

Cassie Chesney Bowie

Cedric and Annissa Ivy

Celeste Margaret English

Charles Curtis Avery

Charles James Fowler

Charles Ivy

Charles Anthony Fowler

Charlie and wife, Erma Lee Walker Fowler

Chaunda Nash and Taylor Smith

Cher LaDina Wallace

Christopher Juwan Fowler

Christopher Garza

Consuelo Reed

Churley Gene Fowler Moore

Creighton **Dejuan** Wallace

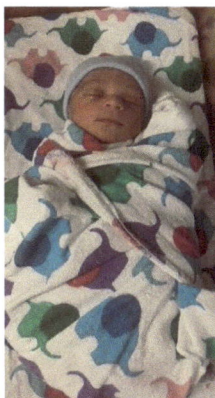

Damian Rachard Caldwell   Dean Royce Caldwell   Danae Inez Caldwell   Darcy Lydell Nash

D'Andre Pittman, son, Austin Carter & wife, Kesha   Davonte Daniel & brother, DAndre Pittman

Dinita Inez Mack Caldwell   D'Juana Valentine Hawkins   Eliece Hawkins   Elizabeth L. Williams Phillips

Elois Bowie Payton   Ethan Hawkins   Dr. Gabriella Caldwell Miller, PhD

Frances Jeanette Mayweather Nash

Gabriel Garcia

Garrett Garcia

Garlean Wilson Johnson

Gwen Bowie

Hudson Caldwell, Sr.

Hudson (Hearter) Caldwell, Jr.

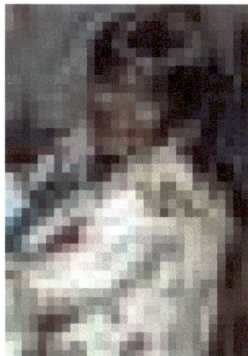

Ida Mae Fowler Smith

Irene Caldwell

Irene Fowler

Erma Lee Walker Fowler and Ramona Fowler

James & Elizabeth Phillips

Jessie James Bowie

James P. Bowie

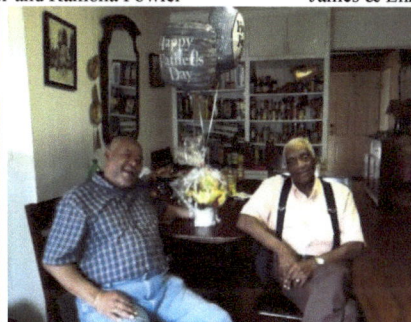

James Earl Nash & his Dad, Joe Nash

Jayden Christopher Byrd

Jamal Caldwell

JC Wilson

Janice Annette Byrd Rice

JaNya Miller

Jasmine Renae Rice

Jazmine Bowie

Jay Thornton

Jessie Mae Lewis

Jo Ann Nash

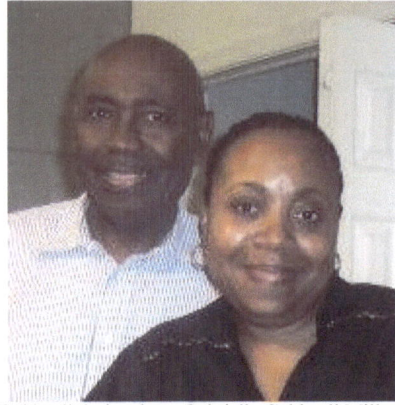

John Thomas Caldwell & daughter, Gabriella Caldwell Miller

Joie Thornton

John Michael Fowler & daughter

Jonae Corlis Lyons

Joshua Fowler

Joslyn Fowler Robinson

Joy Caldwell

Jurlean (Jewl) Fowler Avery

Kamilah Kay Mabrey & son, Keil Dread

Karmen Denise Byrd

Karsyn Bailey Smith

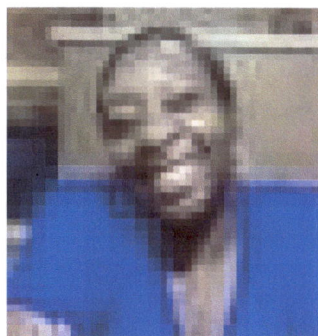

Kathy Thornton

Kyer Dion Bowie

Kya Mabrey

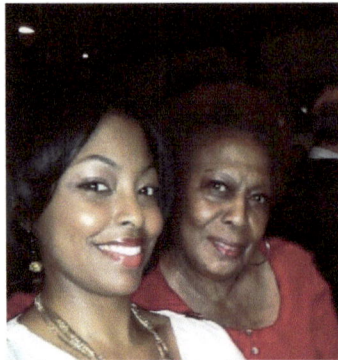

Lachelcia Watts & cousin, Pauline Fowler Brooks

Lamonda Caldwell & daughter, London Ann Scott

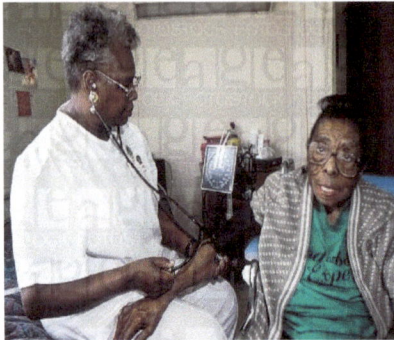

Lanell Bowie

LaQueena LeBlanc Fowler

Lauren Marie Brown

Lexus Zariah Ashford

Leonard Fowler

First Bath!!

Baby Liam

Linda Watts & Pauline Fowler Brooks

Linda Harris Caldwell

Lisa Byrd Minus & Tony Minus

Loretta Bates & daughter, Tameeka Bate   Lonnie Fowler

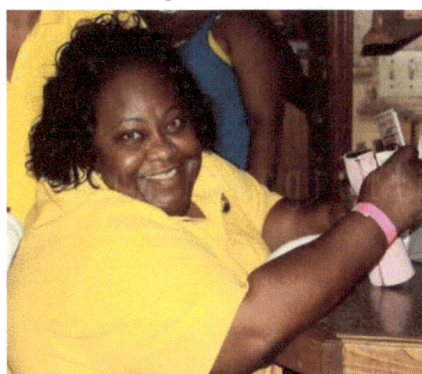

Loretta Fowler Warren Moore   Lorrina Fowler

Malika Jones   Malik Miller   Malikah Mabrey & Leonard Horton

Mamie Bessie Wilson Fowler   Mark Allen Byrd, Sr.   Mark Allen Byrd, Jr

Marquiese Fowler   Marshalyn Byrd Johnson   Mary Caldwell Craig   Mary Fowler

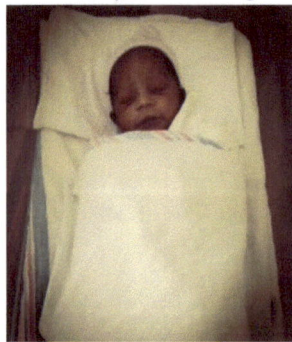

Mary Nash Valentine   Mattie Smith   Maverick Alan Byrd   Mia Kennedi Fowler

Michael Dewayne Cross, Jr.   Michelle Marie Jackson Hawkins   Mya Fowler

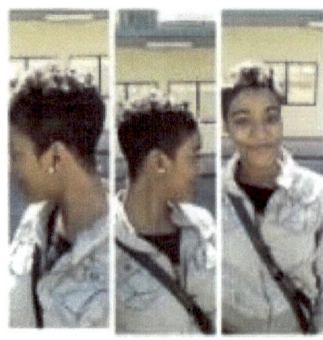

Myles Johnson

Nannie Fowler

Naseer Fowler

Nazaarah (Valerie Jean) Fowler Bey

Neecey Fowler

Nettie Wilson

Norma Nash & daughter, Mica

O'Donald Fowler

Patreka Lewis

Patricia Fowler

Pauline Fowler Brooks & husband, Eugene Brooks

Pirleaner Fowler Evans

Portia Caldwell Thompson

Porsche Thornton

Raelon Reed

Quamaine Byrd

Quaniqua Byrd

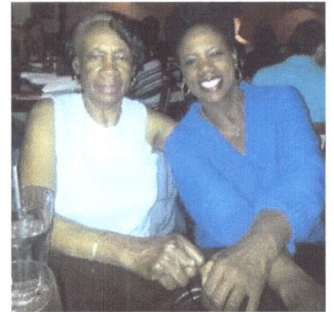

Ramona Fowler & Erma Lee Walker Fowler

Rodrick W. Pikes

Robert Valentine II

Robert Valentine, III

Rosie & Jessie Fowler

Roosevelt (Tony) Caldwell

Ruby Lee Nolen Fowler

Ruby Smith Qualls

Russ Fowler

Tanela Fowler Hicks

Taylor Olivia Caldwell

Theodore Henderson Fowler Tameeka Bates Fowler   Timica Miller Fowler   Tommy Wallace, Jr. & Shantell

Thomas Pikes, III   Theresa Fowler McNair Tova Daniel Byrd   Tristan Bates   Valerie Climons Caldwell

Victor A. English   Vivian Fowler Coleman   Von Lyons   Walter & Linda Harris Caldwell

Whitney Johnson   Yazmin Vercher   Yolanda Loud Garza

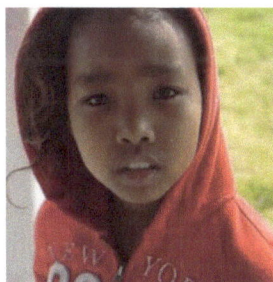

More Faces of Hope

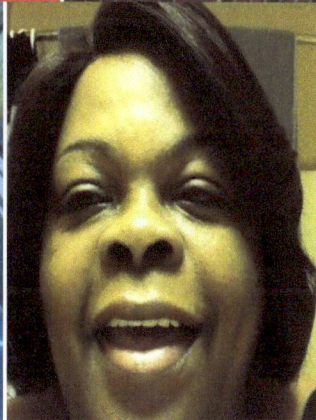

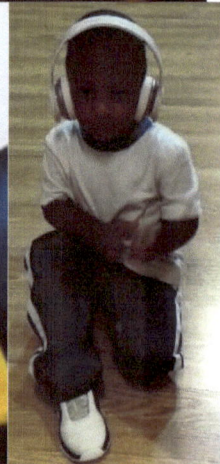

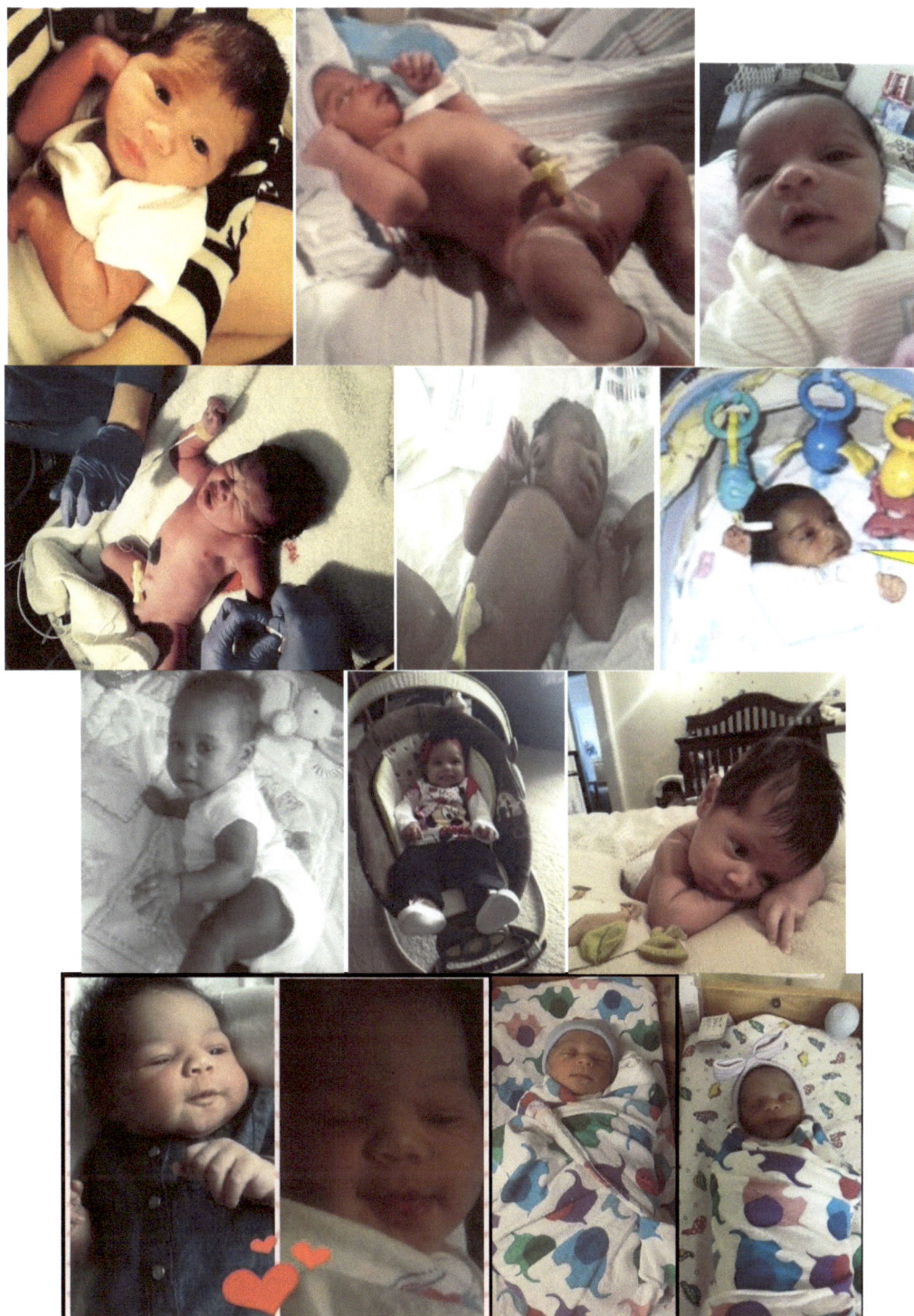

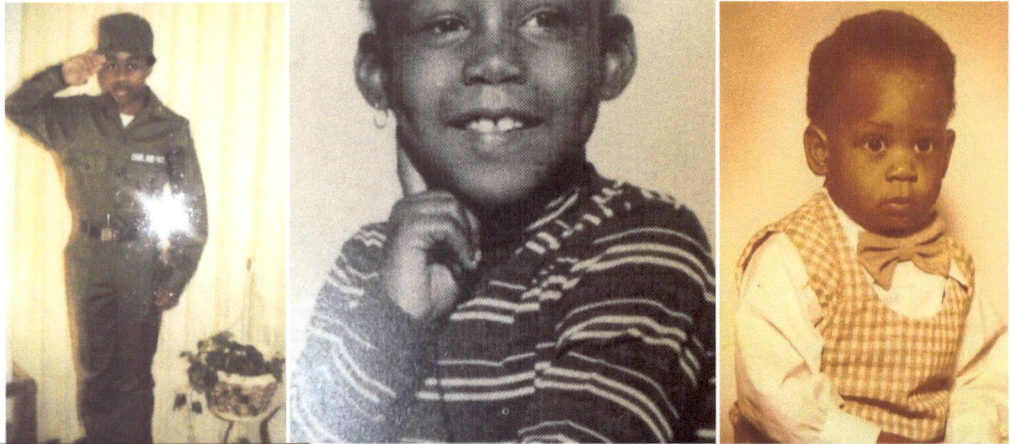

Grandaddy's Princess 👑

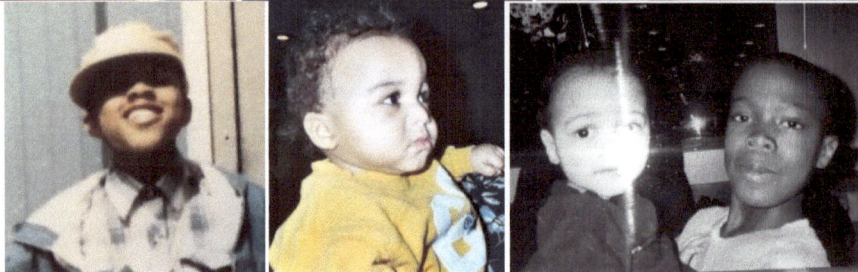

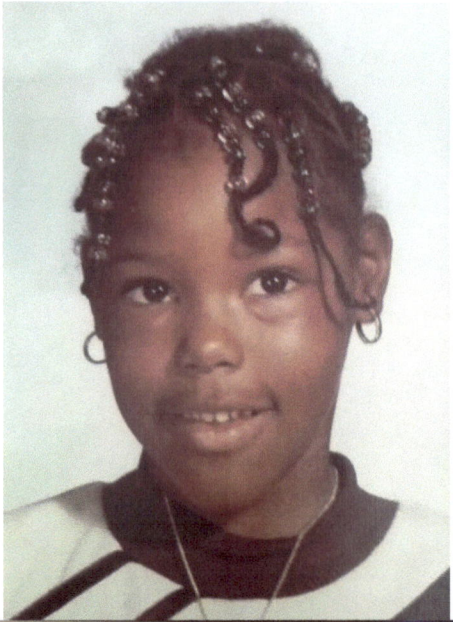
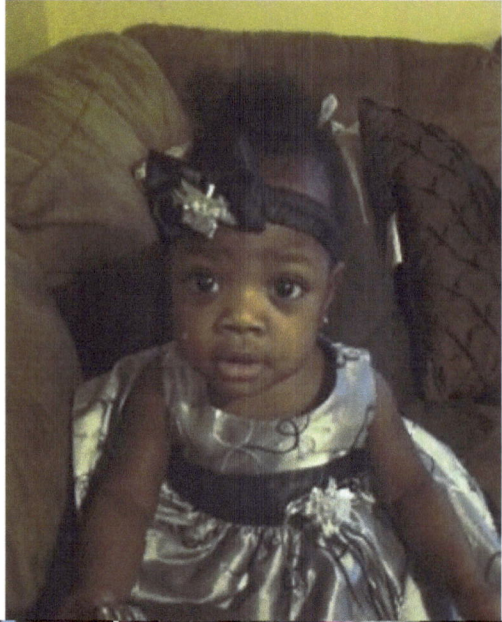

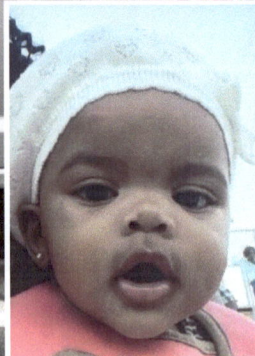

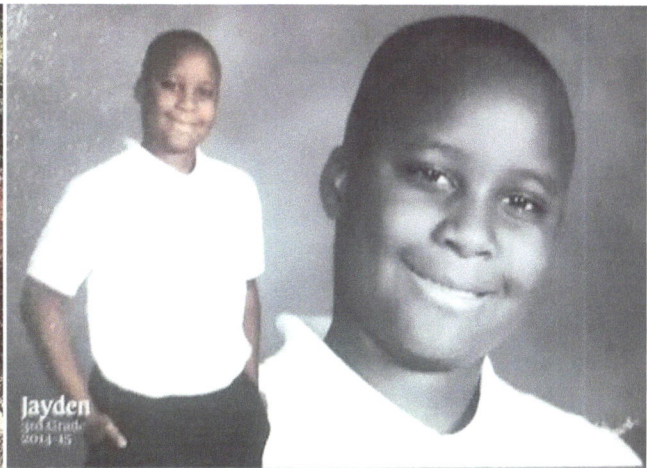

FAMILY NOTES

FAMILY NOTES

FAMILY NOTES

FAMILY NOTES

REFERENCES

1. A History of the Phillips School, by Stafford Davis, April 2000, http://files.usgwarchives.net/la/winn/history/schools/schphi00.txt,The USGenWeb Project, Louisiana Archives Index

2. Amazing Grace by John Newton, 1779, http://en.wikipedia.org/wiki/Amazing_Grace

3. ANCESTRY.COM, http://trees.ancestry.com/tree/family/searchallrecords/message boards (multiple access from 2009 thru 2015)

4. "At the heart of every man's story.....", Wisdom For The Heart, http://www.wisdomonline.org/

5. Behind the Name -The etymology and history of names, http://www.behindthename.com (multiple access from 2009 thru 2015)

6. Fowler, Caldwell, Jess/Phillips, Wilson, multiple family member history, knowledge and memories

7. His Eye Is On The Sparrow, Charles H. Gabriel), http://en.wikipedia.org/wiki/His_Eye_Is_on_the_Sparrow

8. "I did then what I knew how to do. Now that I know better, I do better" by Maya Angelou, https://www.goodreads.com/quotes/9821 -i-did-then-what-i-knew-how-to-do-now

9. If Tomorrow Never Comes... by Norma Cornett Marek ~ 1989, http://www.theribbon.com/poetry/tomorrow.asp

10. National Archives, http://www.archives.gov/research/genealogy/, 700 Pennsylvania Avenue, NW, Washington, DC 20408, Research Card 111802, (multiple visits and access from September, 2009 thru May, 2011)

11. The bitterest tears shed over graves are for words left unsaid and deeds left undone, by Harriet Beecher Stowe, http://en.wikiquote.org/wiki/Harriet_Beecher_Stowe#Attributed

12. The Holy Bible King James Version, Reference Edition, Thomas Nelson Publishers, (multiple access from 2009 thru 2015)

REFERENCES <small>contd.</small>

13. "The name we give to something shapes our attitude toward it."
    by Katherine Paterson
14. "Winn-Then" by, Greggory E. Davies, Winnfield, LA.) Winn Parish
    Enterprise/News-American